Rousseau in America
1760–1809

Jean-Jacques Rousseau (1712–1778)

Portrait painted by Allan Ramsay in 1766. Courtesy of the National Gallery of Scotland

ROUSSEAU IN AMERICA

1760–1809

Paul Merrill Spurlin

UNIVERSITY OF ALABAMA PRESS

University, Alabama

COPYRIGHT © 1969
UNIVERSITY OF ALABAMA PRESS
Standard Book Number: 8173–7101–X
Library of Congress Catalog Card Number: 68–55049
Manufactured in the United States of America

To
Gilbert Chinard
and
George R. Havens

Contents

Preface

IN AWARDING TO JEAN-JACQUES ROUSSEAU A GOLD medal, the Academy of Dijon changed Rousseau, changed France, changed the intellectual history of the world. It had seemed a more or less routine affair—that essay competition sponsored by the Academy. Thirteen contestants had submitted papers on the question proposed: "Had the Renaissance in the Sciences and Arts contributed to purify morals?" Eleven chose the affirmative. Of the two who elected to defend the negative, Rousseau, the "Citizen of Geneva," a somewhat frustrated man of thirty-eight, manipulated the subject to suit himself. He strengthened the indictment by charging that this increase in knowledge had served actually to *corrupt* modern society, thus making his discussion more piquant and more challenging. And his essay was declared the unanimous choice. The Academy, of course, had no way of foreknowing the consequences of its decision, made on a day in early July, 1750. But the outcome was epoch-making.

From that day to this, Rousseau and his philosophy, to which the prizewinning First Discourse was basic, have left few readers indifferent. The man and his writings have been a source of endless controversy and perennial discussion. A staggering mass of books, articles, and essays, much of it highly polemical, has grown up around this provocative thinker. In the writings down the years, especially in those of his bitter enemies and of his fervent disciples—the Rousseauphobes and the Rousseauphiles —it has often been exceedingly difficult to separate the authentic from the legendary, to distinguish fact from fiction. But one thing is indisputable. Rousseau has been highly influential. Harold Laski went so far as to say that "There are not half a dozen men in the history of the modern world who have so ultimately affected the ways of its mind."[1]

Albert Schinz, in his *Etat présent des travaux sur J.-J. Rousseau* (1941), pointed out that while fairly regular "waves" of literary warfare over Rousseau were to be observed from around 1760 through 1912—year of the bicentennial celebration of the author's birth—the trend in the years following this occasion seemed to be in the direction of greater detachment and freedom from bias. It is a certainty that since 1912 many solid and objective studies have been made. Scholars of the twentieth century have brought both the man and his writings into much clearer focus. Space precludes mention of numerous essential studies. Being brought into better focus also is the story of Rousseau's intellectual, literary, and political impact outside France. Books devoted to this type of investigation are, to mention only two, those of Henri Roddier, *J.-J. Rousseau en Angleterre au XVIII' siècle* (Paris, 1950) and Silvia Rota Ghibaudi, *La Fortuna di Rousseau in Italia, 1750–1815* (Turin, 1961). The present book has a similar aim: to inquire into Rousseau's role in eighteenth-century American thought.

My study starts with the year 1760 because it was around this date that the colonists began to be preoccupied with constitutional matters, theories of government, with liberty and rights. The concluding year, 1809, marks the end of Jefferson's second term as president. His election to the presidency in 1801 had marked the defeat of Federalism but the election did not put a stop to name-calling nor did it absolve him from accusations of guilt by association. In the minds of many, Jefferson stood convicted of "the French mania." He was unfortunately influenced, it was said, by "the imported French philosophy." Political attacks on Jefferson, then, may throw some light on Rousseau's role here. Hence the terminal date of 1809.

In view of the illuminating character of the results of my inquiry, it may be appropriate to say a few words about procedure. I have tried to reconstruct the literary fortune of Rousseau in America during this fifty-year span.[2] It is the first undertaking of the sort for this *philosophe*. No claim is made to exhaustiveness. The subject is much too vast and life all too short. The search could go on indefinitely. But one must determine as exactly as possible Rousseau's part in the intellectual life of the period. We need to know rather definitively what he contributed, to use an expression of Jefferson's, to "the harmonizing sentiments of the day." When this is known, one can better assess Rousseau's impact. But even then, because of the ubiquity of certain ideas current in the eighteenth century, great caution must be exercised in making final pronouncements.

The writings of the Founding Fathers, essays, speeches and sermons, diaries, miscellaneous books, university and convention records, as well as private, college and other library catalogs, have been drawn upon. Research based solely upon these materials would reveal, however, only the sentiments of the well-read and of particular sections of the country. I have, therefore, made use of the newspapers for popular opinion.

It early became my practice, when ransacking the gazettes for my book on *Montesquieu in America, 1760–1801,* to jot down references to Rousseau and his writings. Some Rousseau material was probably missed because the gazettes, as I was to discover, often printed paragraphs from various authors to fill up space, without any acknowledgment of their source. In those days especially I could not have unerringly identified passages as being from Rousseau. The newspapers are important sources of information. As late as 1799, according to a knowledgeable eighteenth-century editor, they constituted nine-tenths of American reading matter. Those utilized include the most representative in important sections of the country; placed together in chronological sequence, certain papers offer a rather complete coverage of both North and South during the years 1760 to 1801. Some twenty magazines located in various cities, a good sampling of the total number published, have also been tapped. Newspapers and magazines reprinted extracts from one another. Together they afford a rather accurate cross section of American thought. Data concerning the extent of use of these two media of information can be found in the Bibliography.

My concern in this book, then, is with Rousseau's direct impact upon American thought. I do not, in these pages, endeavor to discuss any indirect influence he may have exerted here through the writings and pamphlets of others. Tom Paine remains a special problem, still unsolved, perhaps unsolvable. And sundry European writers may well have been under the sway of Rousseau. Some of their publications also circulated in the United States. This fact, too, raises the question of a roundabout influence with which I cannot deal in this monograph. The major problem remains that of Rousseau's direct part in the intellectual life of the formative decades from 1760 to 1809, years which embrace the all-important Age of the Founding Fathers. In my investigation of source materials, note has been taken, therefore, only of those passages in which Rousseau was referred to by name. Mentions and citations of his works appearing in foreign imprints in circulation in the United States, unless reprinted here, have also been excluded from consideration.

I have made no attempt to study "Rousseauism" in America. That, of course, is another story. As Albert Léon Guérard wrote in his book, *The Life and Death of an Ideal* (London, 1929), "The history of civilization must consider Rousseauism as a collective phenomenon, of which Rousseau himself was but the representative."

For Rousseau's writings, I have used principally the Hachette edition of his *Œuvres complètes,* in thirteen volumes, first published in Paris in 1865. References to his works, unless otherwise indicated, are to this edition, designated merely by the name Hachette. Good use has also been made of Jean Sénelier, *Bibliographie générale des Œuvres de J. -J. Rousseau* (Paris, 1950). This book is referred to simply by the author's name. A few textual citations have been made to Charles Frankel's edition of *The Social Contract* (New York, 1957) and are here acknowledged. My friend, Edward D. Seeber, of Indiana University, has obliged me with references to Rousseau in Charleston newspapers.

Grateful recognition is given to the University of Alabama Research Committee for aid in a research project from which some of this book stems, and to the Regents of the University of Michigan for leisure hours of work made possible by sabbatical leave. Appreciated also are the aid and courtesies extended to me by staff members of the American Philosophical Society, the Historical Society of Pennsylvania, the Library of Congress, the Library Company of Philadelphia, the Maryland Historical Society, the Maryland State Library, the Peabody Library, the William L. Clements Library of American History, and the General Library of the University of Michigan.

I thank the Board of Trustees of the National Gallery of Scotland for permission to reproduce Allan Ramsay's portrait of Rousseau.

Finally, I wish to express to Professor Gilbert Chinard, of

Princeton University, and to Professor George R. Havens, of the Ohio State University, my gratitude for their inspiration and encouragement. To Professor Havens, especially, I am under heavy obligation for his sustained interest in this work and for his taking the time to read and criticize my manuscript. It goes without saying that I alone am responsible for the development of the subject and for the conclusions which emerge from my study. To these scholars and to others who in their writings suggested ideas and started trains of thought I am much indebted. And last but not least, I am deeply grateful to my wife, Alix, who graciously bore the heat and burden of scholarly creation over an inordinate period of time and ungrudgingly typed several versions of the manuscript. Her price is far above rubies.

P.M.S.

Ann Arbor, Michigan
May 1, 1967

Rousseau in America
1760–1809

1

A Half-Century
of Disagreement

It was October in the year 1794. Through the
streets of Paris moved a strange and solemn procession. Captain
Joshua Barney, U.S.N., was carrying an American flag, leading a
column of compatriots. Bringing up the rear—but preceded by a
book—were members of the National Convention. They were
taking the remains of Jean-Jacques Rousseau to his final resting
place. The book was the *Social Contract*. For the concluding
ceremony inside the Pantheon, the American Minister, James
Monroe, and his suite were the only persons, we are told, who
were permitted to enter the edifice with the National Convention.[1]

At Yale, in the early 1790's, students were greeting one another on the campus as "Rousseau" and "Voltaire."[2] In 1797,
Philadelphians, for a fee, could gaze at a life-size waxen figure of
Rousseau, part of a traveling exhibition. And before long, Stephen Girard, merchant-mariner of Philadelphia, would christen
one of his ships "Rousseau." However dramatic, these early in-
stances of American interest in the "Citizen of Geneva" only
indicate a preoccupation and a concern with the *philosophe* that

had begun long before and which has continued down to the present.

Much has been written about the influence or non-influence of Rousseau in eighteenth-century America. Never-ending study has been given to the origins of American institutions. But even today, scholars still can not agree as to Rousseau's importance to the growth of American thought in the formative period of our national history. Some have believed that certain of his theories found their way into American political ideology, that his theory of compact, for example, had become embedded in the Declaration of Independence. Such belief now stands challenged. But the controversy continues. Not only in the field of political theory but also in the provinces of education, literature, and deistic philosophy as well, there is confusion and obscurity regarding Rousseau's real position in America.

Samples selected from the mass of opinion will illustrate some of the conflicting points of view. John Morley declared that "the Americans took the ideas and the phrases of their great charter" from the writings of Rousseau.[3] The author of an early American dissertation wrote that "Jefferson seems to have been influenced" by the *Social Contract*, spoke of Jefferson's "usual partiality for the political doctrines of Rousseau," and also of the favorable opinion expressed by James Otis in one of his speeches for these same doctrines. He believed that "the colonies were well versed in the political discussions of Locke and Rousseau" and that Rousseau was influential in the reconstruction of government in Massachusetts after the Revolution.[4] In the belief of another writer, the Pennsylvania Constitution adopted in September, 1776, "was founded on the idea of the 'return to nature' of Rousseau, in whom and his disciples in France some of the Pennsylvanians were thoroughly steeped."[5] In the opinion of A. O. Hansen, "The political documents and tracts of the [revolutionary] period give abundant evidence of Rousseau's influence" and he swayed "decidedly the thinkers of the post-revolutionary period."[6] Vernon L. Parrington asserted that from Rousseau and others there came to Jefferson "the idea of political justice and the conception of a minimized political state. . . ."[7] Bernard Faÿ wrote that "although for the most part, Jefferson . . . appears to have taken most of the ideas that the Declaration of Independence contains from Locke, it seems that the idea of an entirely conditional social contract, as well as that of the absolute equality of all men, goes back rather to an inspiration found in Rousseau."[8] And Norman L. Torrey thought that Rousseau's "defense of the inalienable rights of man and of the sovereignty of the people were echoed in the American Declaration of Independence."[9] In the opinion of C. F. Mullett, Rousseau "appealed to American revolutionists" and "Rousseau and a few others not infrequently found their way into the pamphlets" of the colonial period.[10] Albert Schinz declared that the America of Washington and Jefferson was the first State to follow Rousseau's program in the *Social Contract* and that, in so doing, she "astonished the world."[11] According to Vaughan, the Constitution of the United States "is deeply influenced by Rousseau's doctrines. . . ."[12]

Merle E. Curti affirmed that "Antislavery sentiment was strengthened by the reading of such writers as . . . Rousseau" in the last quarter of the eighteenth century.[13] Another author wrote that "Though Jefferson outlived Rousseau by almost half a century, he remained faithful to his master's emphasis on agriculture as the foundation of economic life, of civic virtue and moral happiness."[14] And Rousseau's work on women [see *Emile,* Book V], stated another, was very influential in the decade and a half following 1760.[15] As regards the impact here of the *Emile,* H. M. Jones, however, was most cautious: "The exact vogue of Rousseau awaits investigation."[16] Both the *Emile* and *La Nouvelle Héloïse* "were evidently in demand," according to one writer.[17]

And another declared that "Rousseau's works were advertised almost as widely as those by Voltaire and Fénelon, though his fiction was better known than his pure theory. . . ."[18] But let us hear the conclusions of others.

In the opinion of Lewis Rosenthal, "The philosopher regnant in Independence Hall was not Rousseau but Locke. The Declaration of Independence is not Gallican; it is Anglican."[19] The author of an article on Jefferson and the theory of the compact does not even hint at the influence of Rousseau on the Declaration. He saw, as so many scholars have seen, Locke's influence on this document.[20] John Fiske wrote that "The mischievous doctrines of Rousseau had found few readers and fewer admirers among the Americans. The principles upon which their revolution was conducted were those of Sidney and Locke."[21] Rousseau, concluded another scholar, had "very little" influence on the American idea of compact philosophy.[22] "There was a time, now happily gone forever," Herbert Friedenwald declared, "when it was the fashion sneeringly to pass by the philosophy of the Declaration with a brief reference to its French origin." And he asserted that "we search the American pamphlets of the time in vain for any references to Rousseau's theories."[23] C. M. Walsh thought that "Probably a score of persons in America had read Milton or Sydney, and a hundred Locke, to one who had heard of Rousseau . . . Rousseau's ideas later acquired force in France because of the corroboration they received from America."[24] Carl Becker decried any influence of Rousseau on the Declaration.[25] Gilbert Chinard wrote that "I would agree entirely with Becker: the influence of Rousseau was absolutely negative, nor does it appear that at any time of his life Jefferson paid any attention to the *Contrat Social*, which is not even found in the manuscript catalogue of his library."[26] Another investigator has written that "Rousseau, far from being an important source of the Declaration of Independence, was a minor figure of whom precious few traces can be found."[27] A review of the opinions of others would only be tedious. Obviously, scholars are groping in the dark for an answer to the problem of Rousseau's fortune in eighteenth-century America.[28]

A solution, however, is much to be desired. Prior and more fundamental matters should first be clarified, matters not primarily of political theory, or education, or literature, or philosophy but of literary history. In a word, one should before all else know the extent of American acquaintance with Rousseau in the formative and early period from 1760 to 1809—decades which witnessed the writing of the Declaration of Independence, the Constitution of the United States, the various state constitutions, the establishment of schools and colleges, the publication of the first indigenous novels, "organized deism"—years of Francophilism and Francophobia. To what degree were the colonists and later Americans acquainted with Rousseau's writings? What did they think of his ideas and theories? What use did they make of them? Allegations and denials of influence can have no validity until such basic queries are satisfactorily answered. In the following chapters, I present the findings of very extensive research undertaken with a view to resolving these fundamental questions.

2

Books for
the General Reader

THE COLONISTS AND LATER AMERICANS HAD A FAIR opportunity to purchase Rousseau's books, in English, at the bookshops. *La Nouvelle Héloïse* first appeared early in 1761. *Eloisa,* a translation, was advertised in Philadelphia in the same year, according to findings of a study made by Howard Mumford Jones to which I shall refer later. In 1762, Annapolis and Boston newspapers printed elaborate advertisements of an English translation of the novel in four volumes.[1] It was offered for sale in Williamsburg, Virginia, in 1765[2] and in Baltimore certainly in 1795 and 1808.[3] *Du Contrat Social ou Principes du Droit Politique* first came from the press in 1762. It was soon available in translation. "Rousseau's Treatise on the Social Compact, or the Principles of Political Law" was advertised in Boston in 1764.[4] In another Boston newspaper in 1793, the *Social Contract* was listed in an announcement of a Dublin bookseller, who proposed to supply American dealers, through a local agent, with books of all sorts.[5] The *Contract* was available in 1796 at Boston's "Salem Book-Store and Circulating Library."[6] It was also advertised for sale in the *Newport Mercury* in August, 1797.[7] The original edition of *Emile ou de l'Education* also appeared in 1762, very shortly after the publication of the *Contrat social*. *Emile* was available in English to Williamsburg readers as early as 1765,[8] to Bostonians in 1771 and 1785,[9] to the citizens of Providence in May, 1781,[10] to Philadelphians in 1792,[11] and to Baltimore readers in 1794, 1795 and 1808.[12] Editions of the author's *Works* and *Miscellaneous Works* were obtainable in various American centers.[13] And so were editions in English of his *Confessions*.[14] Without specifying titles, Daniel Boinod gave notice that he had books by Rousseau for sale at his bookshop in Philadelphia in 1784.[15] And in 1795, Moreau de Saint-Méry, another Philadelphia bookseller, published an extensive catalog of books for sale in which several Rousseau items were included.[16] Advertisement in the newspapers of minor writings was rare indeed.[17]

Howard Mumford Jones has devoted two articles to sales advertisements of French books which appeared in New York and Philadelphia newspapers in the last half of the eighteenth century. Inasmuch as I have not examined New York papers and since a check of my own findings with those of Jones for Philadelphia newspapers reveals no duplicated items, it is appropriate to set forth in this place the results of Jones's examination as regards Rousseau. The files of newspapers for both cities that he examined are by no means complete but he pointed out that they were fullest in the seventies, eighties, and nineties. In each of his articles only the first appearance of an advertisement was noted. In the conclusion of his study on New York papers, he wrote: "The leading authors, in the order in which works by them or about them appear, are by a rough count . . . Voltaire, 30; Rousseau, 11. . . . Aside from the striking preponderance of Voltaire items, perhaps the most significant fact in this list is that Rousseau is no more important than are Fénelon and Le Sage—a truth which should give us pause when next we read brilliant generalizations about Rousseau's direct influence in America."[18]

Concerning his Philadelphia findings, Jones said: "To judge

by the advertisements, the most widely read, the most continuously popular eighteenth-century French author was Voltaire with about 45 separate entries distributed equally (in proportion to the available newspapers) over the half-century. The next most popular was Rousseau with 35, also distributed equally. . . . The number of Rousseau items is especially important. . . . It would seem safe to conclude, therefore, that the vogue of Rousseau in Philadelphia was greater than his vogue in New York."[19]

As regards the South, according to an authority on the literature of this region, few indeed were the advertisements of books by Rousseau in the years 1765–1789.[20]

This survey of the books by Rousseau that were offered for sale in American cities in the last half of the eighteenth century,[21] though unavoidably detailed, makes no claim to being exhaustive. Such findings are necessarily relative. But certainly they constitute a fair sample, from which certain rather definite convictions emerge. In the first place, it is quite obvious that a reading knowledge of French was not at all necessary if one wished to read Rousseau. The booksellers' notices reveal a preponderance of his writings available in English translation. A second fact is the rather wide geographical and chronological distribution of Rousseau offerings. A third and very important point to note concerns the Rousseau titles most advertised. The exact significance of book advertisements in the public press, then as now, is a legitimate subject for speculation. With particular reference to American colonial newspapers, the following argument, however, has been advanced: "Such advertisements indicate the taste of the reading public more accurately than do catalogues of private libraries, which represent individual preferences."[22] If this be so, the results yielded by this survey are most revealing. Limiting the count strictly to the dealers' advertisements of Rousseau's major writings in eighteenth-century newspapers, I find that the data disclose approximately twenty-one separate offerings of the *Emilius,* at least eighteen of the *Eloisa,* and not more than seven of the *Social Contract.* There were also about half a dozen advertisements of the *Confessions* and at least fourteen of *Works* and *Miscellaneous Works.* It is of particular interest to learn that *La Nouvelle Héloïse* was available in English translation in Philadelphia in 1761, the very year of its original publication in French. And the rarity of advertisements announcing the *Social Contract* is especially significant.

The circulating library was also an agency in the dissemination of Rousseau's writings. In Providence, in 1789, a circulating library advertised "Rousseau's *Emillius and Sophia.*"[23] Hocquet Caritat opened such a library in New York in 1797 and the catalog of his library, published in 1804, listed these books in English: the Second Discourse, *Social Contract, Eloisa* and *Emilius.* In French, the *Contrat social, Emile, Mélanges* and *La Nouvelle Héloïse* were available.[24]

Mention, moreover, should be made of the use of Rousseau by compilers of anthologies published in this country. In Philadelphia, Robert Bell produced in 1784 a brochure entitled *Illuminations for legislators, and for sentimentalists.* This contained fifteen pages of extracts from the French writer. In 1792, Joseph Nancrède brought out for Harvard students *L'Abeille Françoise.* Rousseau is ahead of all others in the number of extracts, diverse and often lengthy, herein incorporated. In 1796 and 1797, Michel Martel published in New York his *Elements.* Intended as a text, this book utilized more than one passage from Rousseau. The Genevan was also quoted in Mathew Carey's, *The School of Wisdom* (Philadelphia, 1800).

Three major works of Rousseau, the *Eloisa,* the *Confessions,* and the *Social Contract,* were reprinted in America near the close of the eighteenth century. The *Eloisa* appeared in Philadelphia in 1796.[25] This same year, the *Confessions* were published in New

York.[26] And in 1797 there was published in Albany *A Disserta-tion on Political Economy: To which is added, A Treatise on the Social Compact; or, the Principles of Politic Law.*[27] This was, investigation discloses, "the first American Edition" of the *Social Contract,* as its editors proudly called it. For while it is true that two other American imprints of this epoch-making work, in French and Spanish, have been pointed out in the past, they are in all probability fictitious imprints.[28] Fictitious perhaps likewise was a Spanish edition of the Second Discourse, bearing the imprint of Charleston and dated 1803.[29] Note should also be taken of a fictitious Philadelphia imprint entitled *Les Bigarures d'un citoyen de Genève,* incorrectly attributed to Rousseau in a newspaper advertisement of a Philadelphia bookdealer in 1783.[30] Another work, regularly but falsely ascribed to Rousseau,[31] was the *Letters of an Italian Nun and an English Gentleman.* This book had several American editions,[32] further tributes to Rous-seau's fame.

3

American Acquaintance
with Rousseau

THE ENLIGHTENMENT, LIKE THE RENAISSANCE, WAS
no localized phenomenon. Eighteenth-century France was, of
course, its principal theater. But the vast movement of ideas that
the expression suggests stopped at no frontiers and rolls on
unchecked even today. As members of the "Atlantic community"
Americans were subject to the same general climate of ideas that
brought about the Enlightenment in Europe. The Age of the
Founding Fathers was the Age of Enlightenment with a slight
time lag. Franklin and Jefferson were transatlantic *philosophes.*
Some scholars, nevertheless, have been inclined to look upon
eighteenth-century America as a hermetically-sealed island, as if
it were not "a peece of the Continent, a part of the maine." But it
is already evident that readers of newspapers could hardly have
failed to note Rousseau's name so constantly recurring in the
booksellers' lists published in the gazettes. This, however, is of
little importance. What is significant is to have some notion of
the extent to which colonists and later Americans were acquainted with Rousseau and his writings. Was he much known
to the so-called general reader? Who were the people who had
some sort of acquaintance with the writer and with his books? I

propose in this chapter to probe this question of American familiarity with Rousseau. The labyrinthine past will never produce an
entirely satisfactory answer, but information pointing to an answer can be obtained from a number of sources. Among these are
newspapers and magazines, the most popular forms of reading
matter. More importantly, one can examine the holdings of the
libraries of that day to see what light they may be able to throw
on the matter. Offered here is evidence gleaned in various places,
especially from newspapers, magazines and many libraries. I have
no intention of abusing the reader's patience by detailing the
many bits of information about the author and his writings that
appeared in the public press. It is important only to indicate
something of its nature, its quantity, and its chronological and
geographical spread.

Information concerning Rousseau filtered into newspapers
from Virginia to Rhode Island and from Rhode Island down the
coast at least as far as South Carolina. He was a familiar figure to
readers of the *Virginia Gazette,* wrote one investigator.[1] In
Rhode Island newspapers of the eighteenth century, no French
writer, according to Mary E. Loughrey, approached Voltaire in
number of quotations or references. "Of those who were mentioned with a moderate degree of frequency, Raynal, Rousseau,
and Montesquieu were about equally well represented, although
the allusions to Rousseau and Montesquieu were slightly out-
numbered by those to Raynal. . . ."[2] In faraway Charleston,
citizens could read a piece "On Self-Murder. A Dialogue in the
Shades" [between Tillotson and Rousseau] in the *Gazette of the
State of South Carolina,* for June 13, 1785. And other Charleston
papers printed bits of information concerning the Genevan.[3]
Here, as elsewhere, much if not most of the information con-
sisted of borrowings and translations from foreign journals.
Newspaper references to the man or his writings spanned the last
four decades of the century, if the examples below can be taken

as fairly representative.[4] It is known that there were about a hundred newspapers published in various parts of the United States in 1790. The newspaper items were varied in nature. There were anecdotes, "thoughts" of the author, fragments and mentions of his writings, accounts of toasts in which he was honored, references to his persecution, arrival in London, experiences in the English capital and even the hymn, in French, sung when his remains were deposited in the Pantheon.

The magazines treated their readers to similar fare. They contained anecdotal material, sketches of his character and so forth. One could even read about "The Last Moments of Rousseau."[5] And a New York periodical, in 1793, ran a full-page reproduction of an engraving of his tomb to be erected at Ermenonville. This, together with a description of it, had been sent in by a reader.[6] Investigators interested in French have made these magazines the objects of special study. They have noted a number of references to Rousseau.[7] Stretched over such a long period of time, the newspaper and magazine items may perhaps strike one as quantitatively unimpressive. But they do show a certain curiosity about and acquaintance with the Genevan.

There were, indeed, many ways of acquainting oneself with him. Americans could "imbibe" ideas of the author from indirect sources as Crèvecœur and Gallatin were said to have done.[8] They could find occasional citations or mentions of him in the writings of foreign authors, e.g., Joseph Priestley, which circulated here. Books from abroad, containing such mentions, were sometimes reprinted in America.[9] Knowledge could come from other quarters. Rousseau's "Opinion on Duelling" was printed in the edition of Beccaria's *An Essay on Crimes and Punishments* published by R. Bell in Philadelphia in 1778.[10] A pamphlet, "Rousseau, J. J. The Gospel of Reason" [an extract from *Emile*, according to Sénelier, p. 122], dated 1795, appeared in *Political curiosities,* a collection of pamphlets published in London for

Richard Henry Lee and which bore the imprint of Philadelphia.

There is other evidence of acquaintanceship. Rousseau is reported to have sent a copy of Voltaire's *Le Siècle de Louis XIV* to Dr. George Gilmer, of Virginia.[11] In 1779, Benjamin Franklin, while in France, was invited to subscribe to a monument to "honor Virtue in the person of J. J. Rousseau of Geneva."[12] Peter Du Ponceau, who became an American citizen and a lawyer, wrote that Mrs. John Craig, of Philadelphia, "would call me her *Jean Jacques Rousseau,* alluding, no doubt, to the foibles, and not to the talents of that great man, and still less to his vices."[13] Certain remarks of Rousseau were a source of some concern in 1787 to William Short, a Virginian and Jefferson's secretary in France. A letter of Rousseau having fallen into his hands, Short was perturbed by its author's comment on the hostile attitude of the people of Montpellier toward foreigners. He wrote from Paris to convey this information to Jefferson, should he go to Montpellier. Jefferson replied from Marseilles, making light of Rousseau's remarks.[14] In December, 1795, or shortly after, Paul Bentalou, of Baltimore, wrote as follows to his friend, Stephen Girard, Philadelphia shipowner: "I strongly advise you to christen the next one you are going to build 'Le *Jean Jaques or John James.'* Under the auspices of such a sage I predict the greatest success."[15] And in 1801, J. S. Watson, a student at the College of William and Mary at Williamsburg in Virginia would write this to his brother: "Upon the subject of politicks . . . I feel the necessity of Historical information. A man by reading the works of Rousseau, Locke, and Paine, may certainly acquire important ideas upon the subject. But here he is always obliged, in a measure, to take the [their?] ideas."[16] Watson's letter touches on a question of greatest significance to this chapter devoted to acquaintance with Rousseau. Who were the men who read Rousseau's works? The answer of the libraries is most telling and it is to these that I now turn.

It is difficult, often impossible, to learn what books were available in private libraries in eighteenth-century America. Indeed, one baffled researcher into private libraries in Virginia expressed himself in this fashion: "I have extended my investigation of libraries after 1765 by a cursory examination of some fifteen lists in the *Virginia Historical Magazine* and *Tyler's Quarterly* in an attempt to find at least one work of Rousseau . . . but none has been forthcoming. Indeed, in the 280 books advertised in Williamsburg in 1775, Rousseau is represented not at all, a fact which is striking when one considers that Williamsburg was a college town and that the *Social Contract* had been published for fifteen years."[17] Although this particular research proved fruitless, books by Rousseau were to be found in the private libraries of Virginians, in those of "Councillor" Robert Carter, Thomas Jefferson, John Randolph, and George Washington, for example. In fact, there is ample evidence to show that many Americans in all parts of the country had Rousseau titles among their books or were acquainted in some fashion with him. A brief survey will make this clear.

In 1759, Charles Carroll of Carrollton wrote to his father from France that "I intend . . . to buy [in French editions] their best authors, as for example . . . Rousseau."[18] The author of a study on Benjamin Franklin wrote that "Occasional references in his writings indicate that he was familiar with the works of . . . Rousseau."[19] In 1771, Thomas Jefferson recommended to Robert Skipwith as desiderata for Skipwith's library "Rousseau's Eloisa" and "Emilius and Sophia."[20] John Adams wrote to his wife, from Paris, in 1778: "Have you ever read J. J. Rousseau? If not, read him. Your cousin Smith has him."[21] Among Adams's books were a number of Rousseau titles, including a 1764 edition of his *Œuvres,* in nine volumes, published at Neuchâtel. James Madison's library—and whatever books by Rousseau it contained —was destroyed by a fire at the University of Virginia in 1895.

There is no catalog of his collection. But Rousseau was mentioned by Madison, though less often than some other French authors, according to George R. Havens.[22]

From the estate of a deceased clergyman came an edition of "Rousseau's Whole Works, 10 vols.," which an Annapolis bookseller advertised as second-hand in the *Maryland Gazette,* July 20, 1775.[23] And a foreign visitor wrote that the Reverend Samuel Cooper of Boston sometimes cited passages from Rousseau in the pulpit.[24] Samuel Johnston, governor of North Carolina, had in his library "Rousseau's Works, in 10 volumes."[25] John Witherspoon, president of the College of New Jersey [Princeton], had among his books Hume's account of his controversy with Rousseau.[26] Rousseau was one of the "favorite authors" of Aaron Burr around 1781.[27] Noah Webster "seems to have digested" the Genevan; he read the *Emile* and the *Contrat social.*[28] There are indications, as will be seen elsewhere, that Charles Brockden Brown, the novelist, was familiar with the author of *La Nouvelle Héloïse.* "Casual reference or quotation" to Rousseau was made by the journalist and poet, Philip Freneau, who had at least one volume in English of the French author in his library.[29] He translated "bits of Rousseau and the French radicals" for Americans during the years 1791 to 1793.[30] We shall never know the owner of "A French Library," which included the "Œuvres de Rousseau, 32 vols." and which was advertised for sale in the Boston *Columbian Centinel,* May 24, 1794. Channing "was influenced by Jean-Jacques Rousseau to a degree which has never been sufficiently emphasized. He himself tells of this experience."[31] Joseph Dennie, Federalist and essayist, quoted Rousseau, and "his quotations are not gleaned from anthologies."[32] John Quincy Adams cited Rousseau's prophecy on the impending doom of European monarchies.[33]

When fire destroyed his home in 1813, John Randolph lost "Rousseau, thirteen quartos."[34] James Kent, Columbia University law professor and jurist, had a "Collection complète" of Rousseau, published in London in 1774 and odd volumes of *Julie* and of the *Œuvres posthumes.*"[35] Joseph Story, who was to become an associate justice of the United States Supreme Court and a professor of law at Harvard, "continually quotes Rousseau in his letters, and the peculiar doctrines of this great enthusiast seem to have deeply affected him."[36] Rousseau was cited by James Wilson in his lectures on law at the College of Philadelphia.[37] Charles Nisbet, president of Dickinson College, interpreted Rousseau the moralist in his lectures on "Moral Philosophy."[38] The *Social Contract* was used as a text by Bishop Madison at the College of William and Mary. Of this we have the evidence of students, one of whom in 1799 spoke of reading Rousseau with the seniors, and in 1801 another student at the same college wrote that "In the Political Course. . . . We have read Rousseau. The Bishop has introduced Locke upon Government which we have read also. I have also read Paine's Rights of Man. . . . These three are authors, I believe, the most celebrated, and, perhaps, the most excellent that have written upon the Science of Politicks."[39] William Duane, who became editor of the powerful Philadelphia democratic newspaper, the *Aurora General Advertiser,* in 1798 had "Rousseau on Politics" and "Rousseau's Works" in 25 volumes.[40] Benjamin Rush, signer of the Declaration of Independence, eminent physician and teacher, cited the Genevan in addresses.

Books by Rousseau, as we shall see, were on the shelves of some college libraries. They were also in libraries of other types. The Association Library Company of Philadelphia had the "New-Eloisa" in 1765.[41] The Library Company of Philadelphia had acquired this novel in English by 1770, apparently its first book by Rousseau.[42] According to the catalog published in 1789, this library had added several of his books, in English, to its collection: another and different edition of the *Eloisa,* a copy of the Second Discourse, two different editions of the *Emilius,* the *Social Contract,* and *Remarks on the writings and conduct of J. J. Rousseau.* In the catalog of the Library Company published in 1807, one notes that an imposing number of Rousseau items had been added to its holdings: in English, another and later edition of the *Social Contract,* two editions of the *Confessions,* one of which contained "the reveries of the solitary walker," an edition of Rousseau's correspondence with Madame La Tour de Franqueville and M. du Peyrou and another edition of the author's letters to Malesherbes and D'Alembert, "Rousseau's letters on the elements of botany," plus "Corancez's anecdotes of the last twelve years of the life of J. J. Rousseau," and "A tour to Ermenonville;" in French, "Collection complette des œuvres de J. J. Rousseau. 24 tomes. A Genève, 1782" and a "Relation ou notice des derniers jours de J. J. Rousseau. . . ."[43] Accessions of the author's works to the New York Society Library show something of the same progression but not the variety of titles. The Society's 1773 catalog lists the *Emilius,* the Second Discourse, the *Social Contract,* the "Letter to D'Lambert" and the "Letter to the Archbishop of Paris," all in English.[44] An examination of this Society's catalog published in 1793 reveals the addition of another but different edition of the *Contract,* the *Confessions,* and "Rousseau's Works, 10 vols." These books were English translations. This same catalog also lists "Rousseau's Works, (French) 30 vols." The New York Society Library's 1813 catalog, also published in New York, showed the further accession of a two-volume set of his "Correspondence, from the French . . . Lond. 1804."

The "new Eloisa" was on the shelves of the Charleston Library Society in South Carolina in 1770.[45] A number of Rousseau books were also given to this library "for the use of the College when erected." This gift included *Eloisa, Emilius,* the *Treatise on the Social Compact,* and in French, the 1755 edition of the

Discours sur l'origine . . . de l'inégalité parmi les hommes.[46] A copy of "Rousseau's botany" and another volume of "Plates to Rousseau" were owned by the South Carolina College Library.[47] Rousseau's "Inequality of Mankind" was among the books ordered for the Rhode Island College [Brown] library in 1784.[48] Harvard received a donation from Andrew Eliot in 1774 of "Rousseau upon Education."[49] At the beginning of the last decade of the century, Harvard College had in its library, according to its catalog of 1790, a copy of the *Social Contract* in English and also an edition in French, a French edition of the *Emile,* the "Lettre à M. Beaumont," copies in both French and English of the *Lettre à D'Alembert,* and "Remarks on his writings & conduct."[50] Paradoxically, Thaddeus M. Harris, librarian of Harvard, who published in 1793 "A Selected Catalogue of some of the most esteemed Publications in the English Language. Proper to form a Social Library," included only "Rousseau's *Botany*" in his recommendations.[51]

From the mass of materials marshalled in this chapter, certain conclusions force themselves upon us. First of all, the facts make it abundantly clear that, intellectually, America in the last half of the eighteenth century was indeed "a peece of the Continent," as we have suggested before. More pertinently, they demonstrate that Rousseau was an important intermediary of the Enlightenment in this country. In the preceding chapter we saw that Americans, in the northern and southern regions, had an opportunity to acquire books by Rousseau, starting in the very early 1760's. The data presented in the present chapter provide the means for a look at the problem of acquaintanceship with Rousseau from the point of view of the general reader himself. The record shows that colonists and later Americans, men of high and of humble station in the North and South, had fair acquaintance with the man and his writings. The newspaper references to him began to appear in the 1760's. In both sections of the country they spanned the last four decades of the century. The newspaper and the magazine items analyzed for this chapter were informative in nature; in general, they were favorable, not derogatory. The number of newspaper references to Rousseau would not be comparable to those made to Voltaire but they would not compare too unfavorably, in my opinion, to those received by Montesquieu.

There were, of course, different levels of readers, though these levels were not mutually exclusive. Then, as now, some read only the newspapers and the magazines. The intellectuals bought the books and recommended library purchases. Books by Rousseau were in the libraries of, or certainly accessible to, some of the Founding Fathers. Among these were Franklin, Washington, John Adams, Jefferson, Madison, Hamilton, James Wilson, Benjamin Rush, and Philip Freneau. In addition to statesmen, the author was known to clergymen, editors, professors, students, writers, to men in many walks of life and in all parts of the country.

Rousseau got into the colleges, notwithstanding what Bernard Faÿ had to say on the subject.[52] The *Social Contract* was used as a textbook in at least one college and some of his writings were in college libraries. Books by the author were in library societies and library companies. The Library Company of Philadelphia, as seen, had acquired an imposing assortment of Rousseau material by 1807.

To judge from the incidence of references in the newspapers, interest in Rousseau and his writings increased as the century wore to its close, becoming most intense perhaps in the 1790's, the decade of the French Revolution. The publication in America, to which attention was directed in the last chapter, of three of the author's major works—in 1796 and 1797—tends to confirm this impression. American magazines also reflect this interest in the *philosophe* in the 1790's.

By the end of the century, moreover, there are indications here and there that he had a certain prestige in the United States. We recall Paul Bentalou's comment to Stephen Girard at the end of 1795: "Under the auspices of such a sage I predict the greatest success." And the opinion of the William and Mary College student who said in 1801 that "A man by reading the works of Rousseau, Locke, and Paine" may acquire important ideas on the subject of politics. In 1801 also, J. S. Shelton, another student at the same college wrote this telling sentence: "I suppose it will be considered an act of treason against truth, to utter a syllable to the prejudice of Rousseau."[53]

Similar indications of acquaintance with Rousseau and his writings by all sorts and conditions of men could be multiplied. But such evidence, revealing a closer knowledge of his work, will be reserved for the discussions of individual writings.

4

The First and
Second Discourses

THE GENERAL READER IS FAMILIAR WITH THE STORY of Rousseau's "conversion" on the road to Vincennes. The first account of this significant event, the "oak tree incident," was related by Rousseau to Monsieur de Malesherbes in a letter that has since become famous.[1] He wrote that for a quarter of an hour in 1749 he was dazzled by light and overwhelmed by insights. He glimpsed a host of great truths. And those truths which he was able to retain after his moving experience *sous cet arbre* were later scattered through what he considered his three principal writings: the *Discourse on the Arts and Sciences,* which received the prize of the Academy of Dijon, the *Discourse on Inequality,* and the *Emile.*

The prizewinning First Discourse, a frontal attack on the arts and sciences, was originally published in French near the end of 1750 and in English the following year. It precipitated a vehement and long-drawn-out controversy, a barrage of accusations and refutations. Charges were piled on charges. Rousseau would have them burn the libraries. Rousseau's paradoxical stand was actually suggested to him by Diderot. Rousseau was guilty of plagiarism. What is the part of truth in all this? George R.

Havens, in his study of this first important philosophical work of Rousseau, made a signal contribution to Rousseau scholarship and to a better understanding of the man himself.[2] Rousseau's denunciation of the sciences and the arts was, he concluded, his own idea; the Genevan's eloquent and concentrated attack, and the polemics which followed, were, as Diderot said, only an "old warmed-over quarrel." In spite of its contradictions, its exaggerations, and its weaknesses, there are, as Havens makes eminently clear, many lasting and meaningful truths in the *Discours sur les Sciences et les Arts*. And one of the greatest of these is that material progress, unaccompanied by moral progress, is a snare and a delusion. Of far greater significance, however, than the question of its inspiration was the effect of the prizewinning essay and the ensuing quarrel on the author himself. For as Havens, who believes in the essential unity of Rousseau's thought, points out, his polemical talents were developed; he was obliged henceforth to express his thoughts more succinctly; the way was prepared for the Second Discourse; and Rousseau's *"grand système"* was already beginning to take shape. What reverberations did the two Discourses have across the Atlantic? Our purpose in these few pages is to show what knowledge Americans had of these Discourses and how they reacted to them.

Surprisingly, because of the early date, the "Discourse, lately published, against the Re-Establishment of Arts and Sciences" was mentioned in the *Virginia Gazette* on November 7, 1751.[3] At Princeton, "Rousseau's theory of the degeneration of society was quoted by the grammar school valedictorian in 1783," according to V. L. Collins.[4] John Adams, in a letter to Dr. Benjamin Rush, on July 15, 1789, reacted in rather characteristic fashion: "J. J. Rousseau's Phillippic against Arts and Sciences amused, informed, and charmed me—but I have loved and admired Arts and Sciences the better from that time to this. What an Ingrate was he to employ Art and Science to abuse them!"[5] In the *Gazette of the United States* for March 2, 1795, "Common Sense," in a letter to the editor, utilized an extract from the First Discourse against "philosophy" and "philosophers." It was the pseudonymous writer's opinion that Rousseau "was himself no inconsiderable Philosopher." But generally speaking, the First Discourse seems to have passed almost unnoticed.

The Second Discourse attracted somewhat more attention. The original French edition of the *Discours sur l'origine et les fondements de l'inégalité parmi les hommes* had appeared by midsummer, 1755. In 1761, *A discourse upon the origin and foundation of the inequality among mankind* was printed in London. This was the first English edition but not the first English translation.[6] Copies of this Discourse, as noted elsewhere, were to be found here and there on American library shelves, including a circulating library in New York City at the end of the century. Mentions of this work in gazettes seem to have been almost nonexistent. A study of Rhode Island newspapers, for example, yielded only one quotation from it, and the investigator did not consider this a representative passage.[7] In Philadelphia, the *Gazette of the United States,* on November 19, 1800, printed a portion of an address by a lecturer in New York who referred to Rousseau in language reminiscent of the Second Discourse. If it passed almost unnoticed in the newspapers, individuals referred a bit more often to this Discourse than to the First.

An early and a most significant use of it was made by "A Citizen" [William Hicks] in one of the many vigorous prerevolutionary defenses of the rights of American colonials against England. In *The Nature and Extent of Parliamentary Power considered* (Philadelphia, 1768), the writer buttressed his arguments by appealing to the *Discours sur l'inégalité.* He quoted passages from a French edition on the subjects of property, liberty, natural law, and despotism.[8]

Nathaniel Chipman cited Rousseau and alluded to the Second

Discourse in his pioneering American book on government. Though respectful of the Genevan philosopher, Chipman did not agree that the savage state was preferable to that of civilization.[9] Benjamin Rush mentioned Rousseau in a lecture, saying that he could not accept the latter's opinion that savages could be perfect and happy without religion and civilization.[10] Samuel Harrison Smith quoted the Second Discourse on man's passions.[11]

For John Adams, however, this Discourse was anathema. He owned a copy of the first English edition of 1761, and on this copy he made many annotations. He heaped ridicule upon its arguments and its author. Zoltán Haraszti, who made a study of Adams's comments, points out that he went through the little book late, during the worst of the Terror of 1794, many years after its first publication in 1755. Adams, "in the excitement of reading," wrote Haraszti, "gives vent to his more spontaneous feelings. He calls Rousseau a 'Coxcomb,' a 'Fool,' and a 'Satyr,' whose reasoning at times appears to him 'a Mass of Nonsense and Inconsistency.' Adams cannot understand how Rousseau himself 'could believe his own Absurdity.' One outburst follows another. 'Wild, loose, crude Talk!' he writes in obvious anger; 'Mad Rant!' we read a few pages below; then, 'How ignorant! how childish!' "[12] One of the things which particularly galled the conservative Adams was Rousseau's stand on property. He again referred to the *Discourse on Inequality* and to its author's "wild ravings" on this subject in a letter to his son, Charles Adams, on February 15, 1795.

James Kent, born in 1763, read a great deal of French. I cannot say that the future jurist and author of the *Commentaries on the American Law* read the Second Discourse. But a biographer of Kent, citing the Discourse, wrote this: "Of the modern theorists whom Kent had in mind as believing property to be the source of social injustice, Rousseau was one of the most conspicuous."[13]

The two Discourses obviously made little if any impact on eighteenth-century America. Indeed, there were so few references to them as to make impossible any valid conclusions as to their reception. The Second Discourse was apparently the better known of the two. Except for Adams's denigration of both, one can say that, by and large, those who cited them respected their author, if not always agreeing with him. The lack of interest in the First Discourse is understandable. With a continent waiting to be cleared, without a strong cultural tradition of their own, Americans would hardly be concerned with the problem of the "Progress Gap" as someone has called it, between the sciences and the arts and morality. More puzzling is the lack of interest in the *Discourse on the Origin of Inequality.* The vital concerns here with natural law and natural rights need hardly be mentioned. We find, however, a dearth of references to this Second Discourse and almost no citation of Rousseau on such highly important subjects. One might assert that it was not known. But the work was available in English translation from 1761 on, and a French edition was cited authoritatively as early as 1768. Americans, moreover, were quick to cite any author with whose writings they were acquainted and whose reasoning was apropos. I can only conjecture that, steeped in theories of natural law and the philosophy of natural rights, American readers concluded either that Rousseau's Second Discourse could add little to political discussion or else that he was too doctrinaire. In England the two Discourses ruffled the surface of things.[14] In America they made only minute ripples.

5

The New Eloisa

ROUSSEAU FREELY ADMITTED IN *Le Persifleur* THAT A Proteus, a chameleon, and a woman were beings less changeable than he. As a moralist, he clamored aginst novels. They were for depraved peoples. Yet when he was forty-four years old, he gave himself over to voluptuous reverie and began to write a novel himself, *Julie ou la Nouvelle Héloïse*. Published in March of 1761, it quickly became a best seller. *Julie* and *Candide* were the two greatest *succès de librairie* in eighteenth-century France. A landmark in epistolary fiction, the Genevan's novel is a meticulous relation of the story of two lovers in a luxuriant Alpine setting. Its pages exude sentimentality and the reader is treated to an effusive display of sensibility.

It was a book, Rousseau wrote in his preface—not, of course, with full seriousness—more proper for women than books on philosophy. It might even be useful to dissolute women who have retained some speck of love of modesty. Austere men might blame its publication, consign it to the flames. As a reader, he admits that he might have been tempted to do likewise. Nevertheless, such men were not to his liking. But as for maidens, his novel was another matter. He insisted that the reading of *Julie* was very dangerous for girls. No chaste maid read novels. The title of the novel itself, said he, was a clear enough indication of its contents to warn young ladies what to expect. If they persisted in reading a single page they were lost! But it would not be the novel's fault. The damage had already been done. Once they began, girls would finish reading it. They had nothing more to fear. Whether he was right or wrong, French and European readers by the thousands read with avidity the story of Rousseau's heroine who had yielded to her tutor Saint-Preux, as Héloïse had yielded to Abélard. The passionate expressions of love between Saint-Preux and Julie captivated a public satiated with novels of an entirely different type. *Julie* released emotions long repressed by a climate of opinion dominated by rationality. The novel had a tremendous vogue and great influence. But the reasons for its conspicuous success in France and Europe need not detain us here.

In the New World, literature had long been weighed down by tradition. American culture was inevitably a provincial or borrowed culture, largely English in derivation. This was to be true throughout the eighteenth and well into the nineteenth centuries. De Quincey would have categorized eighteenth-century American literature as a "literature of knowledge" not a "literature of power" or belletristic. The literary winds began to shift only at the very end of the century, with the fiction of Charles Brockden Brown (1771–1810) and a handful of other writers of romances. If at the turn of the century native novelists were few, demands for novels were many. Interest in fiction had been long building up but now was wide-spread. An insight is provided in a letter from a woman bookdealer in Raleigh, North Carolina, in 1801 to one of the country's leading publishers, Mathew Carey, in Philadelphia. "Mr. Carey will be so obliging as to send as many of the Novels as he can procure, it will be mutually our interest to keep a good collection, as the good folks here love

light reading."[1] Her list of "light reading" included an order for
one copy of "Eloisa."[2] Booksellers had met the demand by im-
porting and by publishing novels of English and other European
authors. Parson Weems, who traveled for Mathew Carey, wrote
to him from Dumfries, Virginia, on March 24, 1801, giving an
inventory of books on hand. Among these were "5 Eloisa 3
Vol."[3] The circulating library also helped to meet the increased
demand. In the opinion of J. H. Shera, "the growth and prosper-
ity of the circulating library was concurrent with and in large
measure dependent upon the rising popularity of the novel as a
literary form."[4] Another investigator writes that by the end of the
eighteenth century, the circulating library "had become a mid-
dle-class institution, no longer the property of wealthy merchants, who began to speak of the libraries as 'slop-shops of
literature.' "[5]

The early American novel has received the attention of many
scholars. Studies of eighteenth-century American novelists are
readily available. But of Rousseau, the novelist, the extent and
nature of the impact here of *La Nouvelle Héloïse,* little is
known. Was the epoch-making novel in demand, did it enjoy
favor, did it exert influence? Definitive answers to these questions
will never be forthcoming. But let us try to trace the fortune of
this classic in these pages. As regards influence, however, I shall
have to rely on the opinion of specialists on the American novel.

The "First American Edition" of Rousseau's novel was published in three volumes in Philadelphia in 1796.[6] It bore this
title: *Eloisa: or, a Series of Original Letters, collected and published by J. J. Rousseau, Citizen of Geneva: Translated from the
French. Together with the Sequel of Julia; or, The New Eloisa.*
The novel had been available in English translation since 1761,
the year of its first appearance in French. And American booksellers had early brought it to the attention of the public. "The
New Eloisa" was one of the books advertised by D. Hall in a

streamer across the bottom of the inside pages of the *Pennsylvania Gazette* on January 28, 1762, and in subsequent issues.
Another Philadelphia bookseller, Rivington, ran the following
advertisement in this gazette on February 4 of the same year:

> The New Eloisa, written by the ingenious Rousseau; this is the
> favourite novel; every one who hears of it, reads and admires it.
> Elocution, Sensibility, Refinement and Humour, constitute its
> principal Ornaments, and it is the only Novel that has been
> equally well received with the celebrated Clarissa Harlowe, to
> which it bears some Resemblance, only the New Eloisa is
> allowed to be a more masterly and instructive Performance.[7]

The advertisement of the novel in the *Maryland Gazette* for
December 9, 1762, was accompanied by a column and a half of
laudatory criticism taken from the *Critical Review*. Here was
fiction of much more than passing interest and these particular
advertisements in the Philadelphia and Annapolis newspapers
reflect the fever of an exciting new literary find. Indeed, Leslie A.
Fiedler, speaking of the early 1760's, goes so far as to affirm that
the *New Eloisa* was "the most widely read novel in the colonies."[8] But Fiedler offers no documentary evidence in support of
his statement.

The novel was offered in American newspapers under a variety of titles: *The Modern Eloisa, The New Eloisa, Julia, or the
new Eloisa* and *Eloisa.* It was advertised in the gazettes, as
pointed out in the second chapter, from 1762 to 1808, and by
booksellers from Boston to Williamsburg. And as previously
noted, it was on the shelves of some of the library companies and
societies and available in both English and French in Caritat's
great circulating library in New York City. We have seen too
that Thomas Jefferson had recommended *Eloisa* in 1771 as a
desideratum for Robert Skipwith's library.

This novel was, in fact, in many private libraries. Excluding the owners of sets of the complete works of Rousseau, one can say that a number of men in quite different walks of life owned copies or were familiar with it. Whether or not Benjamin Franklin ever read it, it is reported that the Comtesse d'Houdetot showed him the manuscript of *La Nouvelle Héloïse* which Rousseau "had penned . . . expressly for her."[9] George Washington had in his library an edition in French (Amsterdam, 1773), though the book bears neither his autograph nor bookplate.[10] "Councillor" Robert Carter, also of Virginia, had "Eloisa original Letters. 5 Vol's." among his books.[11] *Julia* was in the library of Solomon Drowne, Rhode Island College graduate of 1773 and member of the Brown University faculty in the early nineteenth century.[12] James Kent, who became a chief justice of the New York state supreme court and whose wide reading in French has already been referred to, read "Eloïse" in 1793.[13] John Randolph, lawyer and statesman who had studied at the College of New Jersey and at Columbia College, declared that Rousseau's "Julie" was one of the books which "have made up more than half of my wordly enjoyment."[14] Joseph Story was graduated from Harvard in 1798. In this year, in a letter to an acquaintance concerning Rousseau's *Emile,* Story urged him to "Read his Eloisa and be crazy."[15] Speaking of the time around 1800–1801, Story's son said that "The strong coloring which his mind received from Rousseau at this period, shows itself in every word he wrote. Disgust at the artificiality of life, and raptures on the claims of friendship and love, fill half his letters."[16] Channing was filled with ecstasy by *The New Eloisa,* which he read about 1799. "I have been reading Rousseau's Eloise. What a writer! Rousseau is the only French author I have ever read, who knows the way to the heart."[17] About 1801, John Adams made annotations on his copy of *La Nouvelle Héloïse* and these annotations, Chinard wrote, show how attentively Adams read the novel and unexpectedly drew moral profit from his reading.[18] A French edition of the novel, published in Paris in 1806, was also among the books of J. S. Buckminster, a New England clergyman.[19]

Eighteenth-century American criticism of French literature is not easy to come by. One small piece of criticism, to cite an example, is the Reverend John Clarke's *Letters to a Student in the University of Cambridge, Massachusetts,* published in Boston in 1796. Clarke praises writings of Florian, Fénelon, the Abbé Barthélemy, Buffon, and Bernardin de Saint-Pierre. But he does not mention *The New Eloisa!* One wonders whether he was offended by it. For in one place and another the moral issue was raised. In Philadelphia, also in 1796, William Cobbett, in notes to *The Bloody Buoy,* reprinted extracts from a scathing satire of Rousseau and his novel.[20] One line of this will give a slight indication of its nature: "this romance will teach how to seduce a young girl philosophically." A few years earlier, the same sarcastic piece of writing from which Cobbett drew had appeared *in extenso* in the *New York Magazine* as a "Satire of M. Voltaire, against M. Rousseau's Eloisa. A Prophecy given 1761."[21] However, the author of the satire was not Voltaire, as was then thought, but Charles Bordes.[22] A remark of Parson Weems, the book peddler, is of particular interest. In a letter from Augusta, Georgia, on May 31, 1810, Weems told Carey to "Send *no more* sorrow of Werter, nor Hoyle, nor Eloisa,—nor any book of bad morals."[23] Other strictures on the novel are contained in the two following bits of personal criticism. The novel was reviewed by a Vermont judge, Royall Tyler. "This romance," he wrote, "like the incoherence of Hamlet, has 'method in madness.' It is a jumble of philosophy and love, and, though the author himself is against me, may be read by susceptible fifteen without danger. Girls will comprehend but few of his pernicious ideas, except the first kiss of love in the grove scene; and kisses and groves are abundantly familiar: no information on this subject can be given by ROUSSEAU."[24] Somewhat more perceptive are these remarks of the Reverend Samuel Miller:

> But, among all the French novelists, J. J. Rousseau unquestionably holds the first place as a man of genius. His *Nouvelle Heloise* is one of the most remarkable productions of the age. Eloquent, tender, and interesting in the highest degree; yet full of inconsistency, of extravagance, of licentious principle, and of voluptuous, seducing description. Poison lurks in every page; but concealed from the view of many readers by the wonderful fascination which is thrown around every object. Of the dangerous tendency of this work, indeed, the author was himself fully sensible, and speaks freely. A circumstance which forms one among the many grounds of imputation against the morality of that singular man.[25]

Not every reader, however, raised the moral issue. Certainly Randolph, Story, and Channing did not. It is unfortunate that more reactions to the novel are not available.

American readers were imbued, of course, with the sentimentalism and sensibility so peculiarly characteristic of many eighteenth-century novels. Readers and writers alike were caught in these two strong fictional currents. In 1782, Robert Bell printed and sold in Philadelphia Henry Mackenzie's *The Man of Feeling* with "A Poem, Originating from Rousseau's Eloisa." This poem, "The Sentimental Sailor; or, St. Preux to Eloisa," covers a number of pages.[26] The *Freeman's Journal* of April 11, 1787, according to Lewis Leary, "contained 'St. Preux to Eloisa,' inspired by Rousseau's Nouvelle Héloïse. . . ."[27] This is a poem whose only Rousseauistic inspiration is its title.[28] Under the heading, "The introduction of Rousseau into the sphere of Sensibility," the *American Universal Magazine,* toward the end of the century, reprinted verses dealing with Rousseau from "Hayley's triumphs of temper." The Genevan's gifts of sensibility, particularly in "Julia," are here praised.[29]

Having found little Rousseau in his study of "The Importation of French Literature in New York City, 1750–1800," Jones concluded: "Undoubtedly, however, sentimentalism is well represented by the novels of Mde. de Genlis, Florian, d'Arnaud and Marivaux."[30] Yet none of these authors ever became "better sellers" in the country at large as did Rousseau. Our purpose is not to emphasize Rousseau's contribution to sentimentalism but to ascertain in so far as feasible the facts concerning the reception here of *The New Eloisa*. Let us take other soundings.

What impact, if any, did Rousseau's novel have on the first American novelists? Some information, but not much, can be gleaned from studies on the American novel. Tremaine McDowell wrote: "Although the general forces in foreign literature which shaped the American novel in the eighteenth century are self-evident, the specific influences which are responsible for its sensibility are not equally obvious. . . . It is probable that Rousseau encouraged emotionalism in America, but he is usually regarded by the novelist as a dangerous being. . . . Mrs. Sally Wood admits that he wielded 'a pen of fire,' but she fears French republicanism; the author of *The Art of Courting* (1795) grants that he wrote 'many things worthy of being treasured up by the female mind,' yet he produced much 'which cannot fail of giving disgust to a lady of sensibility'; and Mrs. Rowson condemns *Eloise* as a 'pernicious novel' which perverts the judgment."[31] Herbert Ross Brown thought that Rousseau's novel was one of a number through which "Sensibility also filtered into this country. . . ."[32] And Frank Gees Black wrote that "In the wake of Rousseau, or at least bearing acknowledgment to his influence," was Charles Brockden Brown's *Edgar Huntly* (1799). Brown's was the only American novel in a list so characterized by Black.[33] A study on Brown's sources, however, gives no hint of any Rousseauistic influence.[34]

The author of a biography of Brown found that in the years 1790–93, "Richardson, Rousseau, and the German sentimental-

ists were his daily companions, and it was in their workshop that
he served his apprenticeship. They were his guides until about
1795. . . ."[35] It is also of interest to note that Brown's friend,
Elihu Hubbard Smith, in a letter to Brown in 1796, wrote "That
the example of J. J. Rousseau had too many charms in your eyes
not to captivate you and incite you to imitate him. . . ."[36] Brown
mentioned St. Preux in *The Man at Home,* printed serially in the
Weekly Magazine [Philadelphia].[37]

That Rousseau the novelist helped to swell the currents of
emotionalism and sensibility here is undeniable. The mechanism
and extent of his impact are not at all clear, however, and are
perhaps unascertainable. Such are the conclusions to be drawn
from the opinions expressed above by students of the early
American novel. If Susanna Rowson, author of *Charlotte Temple, Trials of the Human Heart,* and *Sarah: or The Exemplary
Wife* considered *Eloisa* a "pernicious novel" and was uninflu-
enced by it, such was not the case apparently with Charles
Brockden Brown, "the father of the American novel." He seems
to have been affected by Rousseau. How the latter's fiction
touched other novelists of the early American school is problem-
atical. Not doubtful, however, is the success enjoyed by *The New
Eloisa* among American readers. The mounting interest here in
the novel as a form of literature was in itself a factor in its
celebrity. The sentimentality of Rousseau's novel was another.
Feeling was fashionable. Notoriety is also an element in literary
success. And there are indications that the novel enjoyed a certain
succès de scandale. Puritanism was very much on the wane but
books with a reputation for "bad morals" must have held for
many all the charm of forbidden fruit.

Rousseau's novel, from the very year of its publication in
1761, was advertised in the newspapers until the close of the
century and even later. Jefferson recommended it. Prominent
Americans such as John Adams, James Kent, Joseph Story and

William Ellery Channing esteemed it most highly. It was to be found in libraries of every sort, including on occasion the ministerial. Indeed, by the end of the eighteenth century, the novel had been read by countless Americans. It is difficult enough today, let alone in the past, to determine with accuracy the number of readers of a given book. But here are some provocative facts and figures gleaned from the researches of Frank Luther Mott. From the entire field of French fiction, the novels of Rousseau and Le Sage were the only ones to achieve the status of "better sellers" among French novels printed in the United States prior to the end of the eighteenth century. *Gil Blas* attained to this distinction in 1790 and *The New Eloisa* in 1796. This was success. To be an "over-all best seller" in the decade 1790–1799, total American sales of 40,000 copies were required. And the only book by a French author to get into the "best seller" category before the nineteenth century was Volney's deistic *The Ruins or Meditations on the Revolutions of Empires,* published here for the first time in Philadelphia in 1795.[38] *The New Eloisa* was a runner-up to best sellers like *Gulliver's Travels* and the plays of Shakespeare, and to the best sellers of early American novelists such as Susanna Rowson's *Charlotte Temple* and Hannah Foster's *The Coquette.* Rousseau's novel clearly enjoyed a vogue in the United States.

6

The *Social Contract*

IN THE CONSIDERED OPINION OF CHARLES EDWYN
Vaughan, a highly respected authority, "the *Contrat social* remains the greatest work on political philosophy that had appeared since the *Politics* of Aristotle—the most original in conception, the richest in speculative ideas and the most fruitful in
results."[1] What is the history of Rousseau's epoch-making and
provocative treatise in eighteenth-century America? The last
forty years of the century was the period of the keenest, most
intense and most momentous political speculation in American
history. The *Contrat social* first appeared in France in April of
1762. An English translation was published in London in 1764.
Other eighteenth-century English editions became available.[2]
What then was the fortune here of this classic and how was it
regarded by the "political architects?"

First of all, the treatise was reprinted in America but only very
late in the century. In 1797, there was published in Albany, New
York, *A Dissertation on Political Economy: to which is added, A
Treatise on the Social Compact; or, the Principles of Politic Law.*
In a copy preserved in the Peabody Library subscribers' names are
listed. A count shows some 207 subscribers, not including two

people who ordered six copies each, one person who took seven and two others two copies each. This "first American Edition" of the *Contract* is significant. The honor of an eighteenth-century publication here was not accorded even Montesquieu whose *Spirit of Laws* was first printed in the United States only in 1802. In the "Advertisement" to the Albany edition, there is a statement which may throw light on our inquiry:

> . . . the Editors were induced to offer these Treatises of J. J. Rousseau to the public, on account of their utility as well as of the ready sale they promised. It would be a pity indeed, that this (to which they seem particularly applicable) should be almost the only enlightened State in which they should not be generally read. They are indeed here and there in this country to be found on the shelves of such as have with much pains procured them; yet we find them only in the volumes of the author's miscellaneous works [namely, a London translation of, printed in 1767], many of the contents of which are to us less interesting.
>
> It cannot be doubted that Mr. Rousseau had failings and prejudices, yet they are perhaps more than counterbalanced by the solid excellence of many of his writings, which future ages will undoubtedly celebrate; indeed we have good reason to believe, that in the present age his works have been more generally read and approved of in Europe, than those of any other author. His political works especially, of which these pieces are the chief, are repeatedly referred to by eminent writers on government, and the framers of numerous constitutions, organized since their publication, appear to have eyed them with deference, copied them in some particulars, and made improvements on them in others. Hence their publication at this period is the more proper, that the discerning may judge for themselves how far they are perfect, and how far the modifications of some of them have been actual improvements on the originals.[3]

Can one infer from the statement of the editors of the first American edition that the *Contract* was not very well known here before 1776, year of the Declaration, or before their publication of the treatise in 1797 for that matter? The findings of some writers seem to point in this direction. "Rousseau's *Contrat Social* was overlooked" by the Rhode Island newspapers of the eighteenth century, according to one investigator.[4] In the South, in the opinion of another, "The influence of Rousseau seems not to have been important" in the period 1765–1789.[5]

Booksellers' advertisements in the American newspapers show that in comparison with Rousseau's other writings there was a paucity of offerings of the *Social Contract*. But the American booksellers were only one source of information. Books were also ordered from abroad. Collections of extracts were available. One such was Robert Bell's brochure, *Illuminations for legislators, and for sentimentalists* (1784). This contained excerpts from the *Contract*. Sometimes lengthy quotations of authors appeared in the newspapers and magazines. And of course there were the libraries, good barometers of literary esteem. An examination of some of these libraries of various types throws light on the extent of the diffusion of Rousseau's treatise here.

As previously noted, the book was on the shelves of the New York Society Library by 1773, in the Library Company of Philadelphia by 1789, and the Harvard College library had copies in both French and English by 1790. Attention has already been called to its availability in 1796 at Boston's "Salem Book-Store and Circulating Library." The circulating library opened by Caritat in New York in 1797 had on its shelves two copies of the *Contract*, one in English, one in French.[6] The *Contract* was not listed in a 1773 catalog of the books more frequently used by Harvard students.[7] But much later it was a required text in at least one college. In 1801, a student at the College of William and Mary, J. S. Shelton, wrote in a letter:

> In the Political Course. . . . We have read Rousseau. . . . When I reflect upon the mighty fame which his treatise of the Social Compact has acquired, I almost tremble at accusing him of error. But when I listen to the suggestions of my individual

understanding, I am compelled to declare that I think his work open to most important objections.[8]

It is interesting to note that many years afterward, in 1816, Joseph Cabell wrote to Jefferson saying: "Dr. Smith [John Augustine], president of William & Mary, has desired me to ask the favor of you to recommend a text-book on the principles of government, for the use of the students at that College. He is not satisfied with either Locke or Rousseau."[9]

Evidence has been adduced elsewhere to show that a number of Americans had in their private libraries the complete works of Rousseau. Consequently it can be said that the *Social Contract* was in the libraries of such men as Governor Samuel Johnston of North Carolina, James Kent, Columbia University law professor and jurist, and William Duane, editor of the *Aurora General Advertiser* in Philadelphia. A copy of the treatise, in French, was in George Washington's library.[10] John Adams owned at least one French edition of the *Contract* [Amsterdam, 1762] and two copies of the English translation published in London in 1764.[11] He began its study in 1765.[12] Thomas Jefferson's first library was destroyed by fire in 1770. It is hard to suppose that this library did not contain an early edition of the *Contrat social*. But this is only a plausible hypothesis. We shall never know. In his second library, which was sold to Congress in 1815, Jefferson did have a copy of the *Contract,* published late in the century.[13] Although it is difficult, often impossible, to learn what books were in private libraries in eighteenth-century America, there is presumptive evidence that many other Americans were familiar with this treatise.

The *Social Contract* was cited at rare intervals by influential men and by men now unknown and long forgotten. The earliest citation of this book encountered was made by James Otis in his pamphlet, *The Rights of the British Colonies Asserted and Proved* (Boston, 1764). He quoted Rousseau against Grotius for establishing right on fact. The next earliest quotation of the treatise met with was by John Adams in his "Dissertation on the Canon and the Feudal Law," first printed in the *Boston Gazette* in 1765.[14] Rousseau was quoted on the iniquity of feudal government [see Book III, chap. 15]. Josiah Quincy, Jr. showed familiarity with the *Social Contract* when he cited it on the military in 1774.[15] Shortly before the American Revolution, Gouverneur Morris, observed Theodore Roosevelt, "evidently draws ideas from sources as diverse as Rousseau and Pitt, stating, as preliminaries, that when men come together in society, there must be an implied contract that 'a part of their freedom shall be given up for the security of the remainder.' "[16] In 1776, James Chalmers, under the pseudonym of "Candidus," quoted the *Social Contract* in *Plain Truth* (Philadelphia, 1776).

Noah Webster's pamphlet, *Sketches of American Policy,* was published in Hartford in 1785. His first sketch, "Theory of Government," was heavily influenced by Rousseau. Later, Webster changed his mind. In a marginal note in his hand on a copy preserved in the New York Public Library, he confessed that "Many of these notions, taken from Rousseau's *Social Contract,* are found to be chimerical." And in another margin he wrote that "The ideas are too democratic & not just. Experience does not warrant them." His pamphlet was reprinted in whole or part by various newspapers.[17] Alexander Hamilton, in the outline of a speech on July 12, 1788, for the New York Ratifying Convention, cited "Rousseau &c" for definitions of democracy.[18] James Wilson, eminent Pennsylvania lawyer and statesman, was familiar with Rousseau's book. He cited it in his lectures on law at the College of Philadelphia in the winter of 1790–91.[19]

"Publicola" [John Quincy Adams], attacking ideas of Thomas Paine, quoted the *Contract* in three of a series of articles which were reprinted in the Philadelphia *General Advertiser* in 1791 from the Boston *Columbian Centinel*. Adams took issue with the

Genevan's views on the genesis of the contract. "Rousseau contends that the social compact is formed by a personal association of individuals, which must be unanimously assented to, and which cannot possibly be made by a representative body. I shall not at present spend my time in shewing that this is neither practicable nor even metaphysically true."[20] Adams belabored Paine's dream of a democratic form of government for France, citing the dictum in the *Contract* that this type of government was only for a nation of gods.[21] And he introduced a quotation from the *Contract* on the nature of the acts of declaring war and making peace by saying "I must beg leave to call to my assistance the authority of *Rousseau,* a name still more respectable than that of Mr. *Paine,* because death has given the ultimate sanction to his reputation."[22]

"Peter Porcupine" [William Cobbett] quoted the *Contract* in an attack on Joseph Priestley.[23] There are echoes of it also in writings of Joel Barlow.[24] Philip Freneau was familiar with Rousseau's political writings.[25] On the front page of his newspaper, the *Time-Piece,* he published, on December 8, 1797, ten paragraphs from chapter 8 ["Of Civil Religion"] of the fourth Book of the *Contract.* He introduced the extracts with this remark: "The following judicious sentiments are extracted from one of the most popular works of the celebrated J. J. Rousseau; and it is hoped they will not be unacceptable to our Readers, especially as being in point to many particular circumstances of this country." In his poem, *Democracy Unveiled,* Thomas Green Fessenden quoted and ridiculed basic principles of the *Contract.* "But we shall not fatigue our readers," he wrote, "by a detail of all the absurdities, and contraditions, with which this treatise is teeming. . . . we are every where lost in a jargon of words without meaning, and perplexed by distinctions without difference. He was certainly correct in complaining that his ideas were confused."[26]

Evidence points also to familiarity with the *Social Contract* on the part of some less well-known figures, Alexander Graydon, for example, who cited a French edition.[27] But it is most surprising not to encounter the name of Rousseau in places where one might logically expect to find it. It is significant, I think, that he is not mentioned in Alice M. Baldwin's *The New England Clergy and the American Revolution* (Durham, 1928). Her study is limited to the eighteenth century and the last half of the century is thoroughly covered. She shows that there was ample discussion by the ministers of compact theory. Pufendorf and Locke were cited. But no mention of Rousseau. Did they not know him? Did they reprobate him? One minister referred to Voltaire. Or did Rousseau not have what they wanted? John Witherspoon, in the lectures on moral philosophy that he started giving at Princeton around 1772, did not include Rousseau when he named for his students "Some of the chief writers upon government and politics." He did not mention him in a lecture when he said: "Society I would define to be an association or compact of any number of persons, to deliver up or abridge some part of their natural rights, in order to have the strength of the united body, to protect the remaining, and to bestow others. Hobbes and some other writers of the former age, treat with great contempt, this which is generally called the social compact."[28] There is no mention of Rousseau or the *Social Contract* in Max Farrand's day by day reconstruction of the work of the Constitutional Convention.[29] No mention of man or book is found in *The Federalist*. And scholarly opinion points to no influence of the *Contract* on these papers. The general and analytical index of the standard edition of the debates on the Constitution in the various state conventions contains no reference to Rousseau.[30] These are glaring omissions. But there is one even more conspicuous. It concerns Thomas Jefferson, the "Author of the Declaration of Independence."

In many discussions involving the *Social Contract,* the perennial coupling of the names of the "Sage of Monticello" and the "Citizen of Geneva" excites curiosity. Evidence of this linkage is presented in my first chapter. A couple of examples here will show how the two men have been associated in the minds of some scholars. One writes that Noah Webster was "led away by the popular and alluring philosophy of Rousseau and Rousseau's interpreter, Jefferson."[31] Another speaks of "Jeffersonian democracy, directly inspired by Rousseau. . . ."[32] But many scholars, too numerous to mention here, have been quick to deny any influence whatever of Rousseau on Jefferson. Carl Becker rejected the conception of Rousseau's influence on the Declaration.[33] Claude G. Bowers wrote that "The idea that his thinking was influenced by the *Social Contract* cannot be justified by a single reference or citation." [34] In the same vein, Ralph Barton Perry insisted that "There is no clear evidence, furthermore, that Jefferson had read Rousseau."[35] But let us hear on this subject the opinion of Gilbert Chinard, Frenchman, historian of ideas and himself a biographer of the third president of the United States.

In his book, *Thomas Jefferson: The Apostle of Americanism,* Chinard wrote that "No greater mistake could be made than to look for his [Jefferson's] sources in Locke, Montesquieu, or Rousseau. The Jeffersonian democracy was born under the sign of Hengist and Horsa [Saxon chiefs], not of the Goddess Reason."[36] Earlier in his edition of Jefferson's *Commonplace Book,* Chinard had written that "the influence of Rousseau [on the Declaration of Independence] was absolutely negative, nor does it appear that at any time of his life Jefferson paid any attention to the *Contrat Social,* which is not even found in the manuscript catalogue of his library."[37] Furthermore, "There was nothing in Rousseau which he could not find expressed in a much more logical and plausible way in Lord Kames."[38] In analyzing the *Commonplace Book* itself, Chinard found that some twenty-eight pages were taken up with extracts in French and English from Montesquieu's writings. And Jefferson had extracted and laboriously copied into this book passages in Italian from Beccaria's *Dei delitti e delle pene* which cover eighteen printed pages. But the *Commonplace Book,* this repertory of Jefferson's ideas on government, contained not a single extract from Jean-Jacques Rousseau! Quotations from Rousseau were likewise conspicuous by their absence from Jefferson's *Literary Bible,* which Chinard also edited and analyzed.[39]

I have nowhere uncovered in the writings of Jefferson a reference to the *Social Contract.* One would expect that Rousseau's enunciations of the great principles of popular sovereignty and the general will, his discussions of natural rights, property and governments, would have elicited a running commentary from Jefferson. Instead, a wall of silence. This absence of mention of the treatise is enigmatic, puzzling in the extreme. John Adams, an eighteenth-century Irving Babbitt, raved and ranted against Rousseau. But from Jefferson, no comment, nothing. Why this silence? There are several possible explanations. Either Jefferson had never read the *Contract* and was unfamiliar with its theories, or if familiar with it, the comments he made were either not written down or, if written, have not, seemingly, been preserved. Or else Jefferson may have concluded that the *Social Contract* had nothing to contribute to "the harmonizing sentiments of the day," on which he once said the authority of the Declaration of Independence rested. Chinard and others, as we have seen, disavowed any connection of the *Social Contract* with this document. And Chinard also denied that the *Discourse on the Origin of Inequality* influenced the inclusion in the Declaration of the "pursuit of Happiness" as one of the inalienable rights of mankind.[40] In place of the phrase concerning happiness, one would expect "Property," which does appear in both the Fifth and Fourteenth Amendments to the Constitution. Jefferson's substitution of "pursuit of Happiness" is another story to which only passing reference need be made here. But property does play an important role in the *Social Contract* and the views of both Rousseau and Jefferson concerning property did undergo changes.[41] Finally, there is the remote possibility that Jefferson, steeped in Anglo-Saxon theory, and not taking Rousseau seriously, simply decided to ignore him. I find it impossible to believe that the erudite Jefferson, avid reader and perennial book collector, was unacquainted with the *Contract*.[42] He was familiar with other writings of the author. It is without significance to me that no one has been able to indicate the presence of an edition of Rousseau's treatise in any of his ill-starred libraries. As a matter of fact, he did possess a copy of it, contained in a series entitled *Political Classics,* published in London in the 1790's and to which reference has already been made. But a copy so lately acquired is hardly relevant to the discussion. Frankly, the mystery remains. I am inclined to think that Jefferson was thoroughly familiar with the *Contract* but concluded that it contained nothing of value to him.

It is obvious, from the information at hand, that the *Social Contract* made no tangible contribution to eighteenth-century American political theory. Yet the treatise, in English, was advertised in Boston and Philadelphia newspapers, for example, as early as 1764. Manifestly, from what we have already seen, it had no impact here before 1776 or by 1787, year of the Constitutional Convention. How many leaders, like Webster, believed that some of its ideas went counter to their "experience?" Every indication points to the fact that Americans did not consider Rousseau's treatise of paramount importance. How can this be explained?

Two principles, almost maxims, of comparative literature come to mind. First, a writer or philosopher will have no influence in another country if his ideas or theories are basically the same as those of that country's indigenous writers. Secondly, a writer will not exert influence in another country unless the ground is prepared, ready to receive his ideas and theories. If so, the seed may fall on fertile soil. I shall not attempt to give here another analysis or summary of Rousseau's treatise or how its theories resembled or differed from the writings of others on the subject. A number of such are readily available.[43] In the light, then, of this first principle, let us take a quick look at the record.

It may startle some readers to learn that one scholar could write an entire chapter on "The Contract in American Thought" without even mentioning the name of Rousseau.[44] Discussions of contractual theory, if not commonplace, were not unusual in America long before the appearance of the *Contrat social* in 1762. There need be no cause for astonishment to read that at Harvard Commencement exercises in 1747, a student, "Th. Cushing défend la théorie du Contrat Social."[45] Earlier in the century, John Wise, minister in Ipswich, Massachusetts, championed "democratic, contract theory of both state and church" in *A Vindication of the Government of New England Churches* (1717).[46] But a century before Wise, the Pilgrim leaders drafted the "Mayflower Compact," which was signed in 1620. Indeed, speculation about compacts antedates Christianity, going back to Grecian times at least. And for American clergymen and others, the Old Testament itself was a source of information as regards covenants.[47] Interest in contract theory was reinforced by the reading of European philosophizing on the subject. John Locke's important second *Treatise on Civil Government,* like the first, had been published in 1690 and Locke, to cite only this one thinker, enjoyed much authority in America.[48] But it is hardly necessary to pursue this inquiry further. "By the time of the struggle for independence the contract theory of the state, firmly embedded in American political thought from the beginning, became prominent in its traditional role as an argument for political liberty."[49] There is, then, no cause for wonderment when one comes upon discussions of the social compact in writings of eighteenth-century Americans in which Rousseau's name does not occur. Such was a piece by an unknown writer printed in the *Virginia Gazette,* September 11, 1779; he did mention, however, Hobbes's *Leviathan.* Jefferson, Madison, Hamilton, Nathaniel Chipman in his *Sketches of the Principles of Government* and others can and do discuss the "Social Compact" or the "Social Contract" without any reference whatever to the Genevan.[50] So much for the documentation of the first principle mentioned above. Indigenous interest in compact theory, whetted by sources other than Rousseau, had had a long history on American soil before 1776.

As regards the second principle, Rousseau's treatise cannot, without violent distortion of the facts, be cited as an illustration of its relevancy in this particular instance. The ground had been well prepared. The *Social Contract* was certainly fertile in ideas. Yet the "seeds" did not sprout. The book contributed little if anything to "the harmonizing sentiments of the day." The reader has noticed that there were virtually no citations of the *Contract* before the Declaration of Independence. The book, however, had been available in French and English editions for many years. Now the "political architects" were eclectic. If Rousseau had had something which they needed and valued, it is certain that they would have used him as an authority. And his treatise would have been much better known by 1776. But such was not the case. Eighteenth-century Americans made some slight use of the book but not significantly so. No mention of it has been noted in the important convention records. Few if any references to the author have been found in influential contemporary discussions of contractual theory. There are indications of esteem for the treatise. Opinion in the aggregate, nevertheless, appears to have been hostile.

Rousseau's reputation here in the last years of the eighteenth century undeniably suffered because of his association in the minds of conservatives with the hated French Revolution and its excesses. This fact has to be weighed in the balance. But one must also consider carefully the nature of some of the criticism. John Adams, for example, thought Rousseau's definition of the general will "too mathematical or too witty to be very clear."[51] John Quincy Adams, as we saw, wrote that Rousseau's views on the formation of the social compact were "neither practicable nor even metaphysically true." And Noah Webster finally concluded that many of the ideas in the *Social Contract* were "chimerical." The amount and quality of such criticism appear to have tipped the scales against the Genevan. Jefferson himself did not regard the social compact as "a metaphysical hypothesis, nebulous and lost in the night of ages; it [was] a very specific and very precise convention to be entered into or to be denounced by men, or groups, who remain free and yet agree to submit themselves to certain rules in order to obtain more security."[52] Now Rousseau had written that "whoever refuses to obey the general will shall be compelled to it by the whole body: this in fact only forces him to be free." To many Americans, Rousseau was a doctrinaire. The *Social Contract* exerted no palpable influence on political thought in the United States in the eighteenth century.[53]

The fortune of this book is paradoxical in the extreme. "Man is born free, and yet we see him everywhere in chains," thundered Rousseau in the opening sentence of its first chapter. But ironically, this revolutionary cry was heard neither in America nor in France until very late in the century. The parallel between the situation here and that in France was striking indeed. The *Social Contract* was apparently not much read and made little or no impact in either country before their revolutions began. Concerning the *Contrat social* in France, Daniel Mornet wrote that "it is impossible to discern its influence on the origins of the Revolution. . . . and one cannot gather evidence from the testimony of ten readers before 1789 that the work had made any strong impression on them."[54] Whatever its impact there *during* the French Revolution,[55] the treatise was far from being influential here at any time in the century. In fact, it was the other way around. The American discussions of political theories and compact philosophy called attention to the *Social Contract* of Rousseau.[56] The upward curve of references to this book does not begin until a decade after the Declaration of Independence.

7

Emile

AT THE PALAIS DE JUSTICE IN PARIS, ON JUNE 11, 1762, Rousseau's *Emile* was torn to pieces, then burned. Rousseau had noted in the *Confessions* that members of the high court were heard to say openly that nothing was to be gained by burning books, it was necessary to burn their authors. On the day they consigned the book to the flames, the authorities issued a writ for his arrest.[1] Rousseau fled to Switzerland, but in so doing he jumped from the frying pan into the fire. On June 19, they burned *Emile* in Geneva and issued another writ for the author's arrest there.[2] The publication of the book had caused a great stir in the French capital. Rousseau, and also Grimm in the *Correspondance littéraire,* used the word "storm" to describe the agitation. Bachaumont, in his *Mémoires secrets,* referred to the "scandal" the book occasioned. *Emile* was condemned because of its unorthodox religious views. It contained an exposition of natural religion or deism that was bound to inflame passions. An exposition of this sort would also inevitably kindle emotions in eighteenth-century America, where France was looked upon by many as a nation of atheists and as such often anathematized. The appearance of *Emile,* considered by Rousseau the best and most important of his writings, marked the beginning of new trouble and much misery for its author. His religious views did loom large but they filled only a small part of a very long book.

Emile, ou de l'éducation is a treatise on pedagogy written in novelistic form. First published in French in May, 1762, it appeared in English translation the same year. There were to be a number of eighteenth-century editions in English. Neither detailed description of the book nor methodical presentation of its ideas is required here. Scholars have studied it again and again and the number of monographs in many languages devoted to this masterpiece is indeed formidable. Only the briefest of recapitulations is needed in order to help clarify the American reception and reaction to it.[3]

The long treatise is composed of five books, four of which deal with Emile's education, while the fifth is devoted to that of Sophie, his future wife. Emile, the model pupil, is to be a child of good birth, well-formed and in good health, from a temperate zone, preferably France, and rich. The poor have no need of education. Rousseau distinguishes four ages in Emile's development to manhood. He discusses meticulously the kind of education according to nature appropriate to each stage. Emile will be brought up in the country, safe from the baleful influences of city life. His education is to be eminently practical, not bookish at all. He will be taught to question the utility of all things. The sole aim of this educational program is to produce not a lawyer or a soldier or a doctor but a man. Emile must learn how to live. A single condition is imposed in the learning process: he is to obey only his preceptor, Rousseau. The book is concerned exclusively with the education of the individual. It contains no program of national education. Its teaching regarding the instruction of women was traditional. But Rousseau revolutionized educational theory. He would not push the child. He said that the most important and useful rule in all education was not to gain time but to lose it. He respected and emphasized the rights of children. The happy period of childhood must not be sacrificed to learning the responsibilities of manhood. He would prod the imaginations, not the memories, of young people. He wanted Emile to become a man of judgment—and free. Critics point out his inconsistencies and direct one's attention to those of his views on education which they find erroneous or no longer tenable. But his book was one of the world's great landmarks in the history of pedagogy.

It was what Rousseau taught his imaginary pupil about religion, not his pedagogical principles, that precipitated the scandal of *Emile*. He would not even broach the subject until the boy was at least fifteen years of age. A child's religion, he was convinced, was a matter of geography. And there was no sillier a sight than to see children learning the catechism. Accordingly, Emile must be taught only the religion of nature. For his instruction, therefore, he introduced in Book IV the long *Profession of Faith of the Savoyard Vicar*. Here are some of the basic tenets of this celebrated theistic credo. The Vicar believed in the authority of reason and in a religion of the heart, not in one of dogma or ceremony. Revelation he neither accepted nor rejected. He condemned pride and intolerance. He believed in a supreme Being, free will, the immortality of the soul. Prayer of petition he considered an impiety. He thought that man had an innate sense of justice and virtue and this sense he called conscience. A divine instinct, conscience was the voice of the soul, man's unerring guide, the infallible judge of good and evil. The Vicar concluded his discourse with eloquent observations on the sanctity of the Gospel and a comparison of the lives and deaths of Socrates and Jesus. Socrates died a sage but the life and death of Jesus were those of a God. *Emile* was placed on the *Index* in the very year of its publication.

Rousseau has been enormously influential, directly or through important disciples, upon educational reform.[4] Yet nothing has been written on the fortune of *Emile* in the Age of the Founding Fathers. An old order was then giving way to a new. Change was in the air. New conditions required new ways of thinking. Leaders talked much about what constituted proper learning for boys and girls. They showed a vital concern for education.

No book of Rousseau's appears to have been advertised more often by American booksellers than the *Emile*. The survey in the second chapter makes this clear. It was available in English in Philadelphia as early as 1763, in Williamsburg in 1765 and in New York City in 1773. At one time or another, it could be purchased from Rhode Island to Georgia. The book was on the shelves of library societies. Harvard had it by 1774. Patrons of certain circulating libraries had access to it toward the end of the century. Rousseau was used in anthologies compiled here. *L'Abeille Françoise,*[5] a collection of prose extracts published in 1792 for the use of Harvard students, is a classic example. Prepared by Joseph Nancrède, it contained 339 pages of reading matter and was one of the earliest French textbooks printed in this country for Americans. Albert Schinz, who made a study of the book, found that "Rousseau détient le record des citations; il est représenté par quinze fragments."[6] Among these fragments are a number of passages from *Emile.*[7]

Jefferson, as already seen, had recommended Rousseau's pedagogical treatise in 1771 to Robert Skipwith for his library. Other prominent and less prominent persons were familiar with the classic. It heads a list of books in a pay-book which Alexander Hamilton kept in 1776 as commander of a company of artillery.[8] It was in the library of Solomon Drowne, Rhode Island College graduate and future professor.[9] Franklin wrote from Paris in 1785 that "since Rousseau, with admirable Eloquence, pleaded for the Rights of Children to their Mother's Milk . . . some Ladies of Quality now suckle their Infants and find Milk enough."[10] Benjamin Rush, in his *Thoughts upon Female Educa-*

tion (1787), cited with approval Rousseau's "great secret of education [which] consists in 'wasting the time of children profitably.' "[11] John Adams had in his library a French edition of *Emile* in four volumes, published in 1762.[12] In 1790, in a letter to Rush, he quoted from it a passage in French that did not involve the subject of education.[13] Noah Webster and John Quincy Adams, according to evidence previously brought forward, were both familiar with the book. And so were Enos Hitchcock, New England clergyman, Aaron Burr,[14] Martha Laurens Ramsay,[15] and many others. To conclude this rapid survey with one example, Joseph Story wrote in 1798 to Samuel P. P. Fay as follows: "I perceive by a hint in your letter, that you have read Emilius. Pray write your folio opinion of it. I know you admire it."[16] So much for these specific indications of the book's popularity. Now Howard Mumford Jones, as was pointed out in the first chapter, urged caution in speaking about the influence of *Emile* in America, saying that its "exact vogue . . . awaits investigation." This chapter is, then, an inquiry into the facts. For clarity's sake, I shall distinguish and deal separately with three areas of possible impact: on educational theory generally, on female education, and on religious thinking. Any attempt to separate the first two is of course highly arbitrary. But such a separation will enable us, for one thing, to focus attention on the fortune here of that portion of *Emile* devoted to the education of women.

As regards educational theory generally, Rousseau's treatise on pedagogy does not appear to have been much cited. The findings reveal no particular pattern of interest. Loughrey found only two quotations from the book in the Rhode Island newspapers and "they were not the most representative passages. . . ."[17] It was quoted in an article "On the Management of Children in Infancy" in the *South Carolina Gazette, Supplement,* November 1, 1773. The editor of a Philadelphia newspaper cited the *Emile* on the necessity of a child's learning a trade in order to be self-reliant and independent amid the vicissitudes of life.[18] Burgiss Allison, principal of a private school in Bordentown, New Jersey, lamented with Rousseau that youth "should be made wretched by the tyranny of our seniors."[19] With the few citations previously noted and those contained in the book of Enos Hitchcock discussed farther on, these are all the citations of *Emile* on general principles of education that I have encountered.

Book V of *Emile* bears the title of "Sophia; or, The Woman." This book, devoted to the education of women, exerted a very real influence here, in the opinion of some investigators. According to Mary S. Benson, Rousseau was one of "five writers between 1760 and 1775 whose work on women had very definite and far-reaching American influence, and so merits detailed examination."[20] At the end of the century, wrote H. M. Jones, "academies for young ladies begin to multiply only with the powerful impetus given to 'female education' by Rousseau and the English radical feminists."[21] A sidelight concerning this impetus comes from a contemporary, anxious to see established a proper system of female education. Writing in the *Massachusetts Centinel* for March 25, 1789, he said that "there are not wanting many advisers and arbiters of female conduct, but many of them are inexperienced persons, system mongers, who by a superficial perusal of LOCKE, ROUSSEAU, and other benevolent authors, have taken up opinions frequently absurd and grotesque. . . ." But let us take a closer look.

The *Pennsylvania Packet,* on October 1, 1782, printed from "Sophia" more than a column on marriage and the choice of a husband.[22] The anonymous author of *The Art of Courting* (1795) declared that seemingly the great theme of Rousseau and two other writers was "that the highest ambition a woman ought to have, is to please man. . . ."[23] The author, nevertheless, was satisfied with Eliza's reading Rousseau and the others. In a magazine article in 1797, Rousseau was quoted as saying that "A young girl must be trained up for a husband, like an eastern beauty for a harem."[24] The writer was sarcastic in his use of this quotation. The author of "Sophia" had drawn the fire of the English feminist, Mary Wollstonecraft. She in turn was attacked by the Reverend Richard Polwhele whose poem, *The Unsex'd Females,* Cobbett reprinted in New York in 1800. The poem contained references to and a quotation from Rousseau.[25] The *Columbian Centinel* reproduced a part of this poem on June 21, 1800. In the same paper on July 9, a female reader rose to the defense of the English feminist, cited Rousseau on the education of women and a rejoinder to him by Mrs. Wollstonecraft. William Bentley, a minister, paid tribute to the penetration of the Genevan who, "with all his indiscretions," stressed the importance of early associations and education for contentment. He quoted Book V on the peace of domestic life.[26] The *Lady's Weekly Miscellany* also quoted from this book a paragraph in which woman's speech was eulogized.[27]

Anthologies aside, the centerpiece, as regards numbers of references to the *Emile,* is the *Memoirs of the Bloomsgrove Family,* published in two volumes in Boston in 1790.[28] The author was Enos Hitchcock, a Harvard graduate of 1767 and a New England clergyman. One investigator has called this work "the second American novel to be published in book form—if the term novel may be accurately applied to it."[29] It was "the longest American work dealing with women which appeared before 1800," according to another.[30] Hitchcock cited the *Emile* in a number of passages.[31] His citations were eclectic. They were not confined to "Sophia" or any other single book in the masterpiece. His *Memoirs* can hardly be considered a treatise devoted exclusively to the education of females. He quoted Rousseau approvingly on a variety of points. He could not, however, accept the Genevan's views that a boy should not be taught anything before the age of twelve or that religious instruction should be post-poned until the age of fifteen or eighteen.[32] Hitchcock respected Rousseau as an authority on education. "I beg leave," he said at one point in his book, "to advance under the standard of Lord Kaimes [*sic*] and Rousseau." But he could also be critical of the latter. From my own study of Hitchcock's *Memoirs,* I sense that their author was more under the sway of Kames than Rousseau. So much for the use here of Book V, as evidenced by the citations of Hitchcock and others.

In both France and Geneva, anathema had been pronounced against Rousseau for his views on religion, expressed most me-thodically in Book IV of *Emile.* There remains to be considered in this chapter the impact of these views on religious thinking here. His "infidel" philosophy, as some called it, aroused much antagonism in Protestant America. He became a target, as did other *philosophes,* for the devastating fire of pamphleteers and sermonizers. Here are samples of attitudes held by many. Rous-seau, declared one of the magazine editors, was "an enemy." His lips, in the words of a president of Union College, were "the lips of infidelity itself." Sharp-tongued Timothy Dwight, president of Yale from 1795 to 1817, attacking "French philosophy," wrote that religion in America had suffered much in the Revolutionary War. It was then that Americans had intercourse with "French-men; disciples of Voltaire, Rousseau, D'Alembert, and Diderot; men, holding that loose and undefined Atheism. . . ."[33] William Livingston, governor of New Jersey, in a piece called "Thoughts on Deism," wrote a defense of Christianity. He spoke sarcasti-cally of the "wretched pun or threadbare jest of a Voltaire, or a Rousseau" as regards the proofs of this religion.[34] William Cob-bett asserted that the Genevan had "exhausted all the powers of his fascinating eloquence in the cause of anarchy and irreli-gion."[35] A writer in the *Gazette of the United States* for July 12, 1800, maintained that "He, who directs the willing pupil to one

Roman or Grecian author, and confirms the faith and regulates the passions of youth by pointing to the Bible, and to the ancient and settled and salutary system of morals, is in the sight of God, and of sober and considerate man of more value to society, than all the Voltaires, the Rousseaus, and the Condorcets. . . ." In 1803, a weekly magazine, the *Balance and Columbian Repository* (Hudson, New York), ran in five consecutive numbers a "Profession of Philosophic Faith. Translated for the *Balance,* from the French of a Pupil of Rousseau." In an editorial introductory note to the first number, one finds this: "How much is it to be lamented, that a man of such genius—the author of an admirable system of education, and of excellent reflections on human life and manners, should likewise be the author of sentiments which declare religion as fit only for despots and slaves—inconsistent with the happiness of civil society—of sentiments which favour licentiousness and the commission of the worst crimes."[36] In the "Profession," anti-philosophical, the Pupil satirizes the sophistry of his master. The translator feared the effect of Rousseau's religious views on young people and by his translation he hoped to warn them and "the votaries of religion and humanity . . . against the infection of that subtile and dangerous poison. . . ." But if Rousseau's deism was damned by many, it was also praised.

His most fervent American advocate perhaps was Elihu Palmer who, according to James Carnahan, one-time president of the College of New Jersey (Princeton), "was brought to Newburgh [ca. 1799 by "The Druid Society"] under a promise of an annual salary, to detail from Sabbath to Sabbath the opinions of Voltaire, Paine, Rousseau, Godwin, and others of the same stamp."[37] Palmer cited Rousseau with approval in his *Principles of Nature* (1802). But he did much more than this. In his magazine, *Prospect* (New York City), Palmer, in 1804, printed almost *in extenso* the "Profession of Faith of a Savoyard Curate, from Rousseau." He made these remarks in introducing the first extract: "This work has had very little circulation in this country, and from the known reputation of Rousseau, as a writer as well as the internal excellence of the work itself, it is presumed it will be favorably received by all our subscribers. . . . There is however in this small work, such profound reflection and such sentiments of virtue as justly entitle it to a high share of estimation in the minds of virtuous and Philosophic men."[38]

On the subject of religion, the Genevan had his disciples and admirers but his opponents and detractors appear to have weighed more heavily on the scales. If he was excoriated for his deistic beliefs by Dwight, Cobbett, and a host of others, Rousseau, nevertheless, appealed religiously to the hearts and minds of many. I refer particularly to the deep impression made on Americans by a very eloquent passage in the *Profession of Faith of the Savoyard Vicar,* in which Socrates is compared to the son of Mary and where the author exclaims: "if Socrates lived and died like a philosopher, Jesus lived and died like a God." Here are its opening and closing lines:

> I acknowledge to you, that the majesty of the scriptures astonishes me, and the sanctity of the gospel fills me with rapture. Look into the writings of the philosophers, with all their pomp and parade; how trivial they appear, when compared to this sacred volume. Is it possible, that a book so simple and yet so sublime, should be the work of man?. . . . Shall we say that the evangelical history was invented at pleasure? My friend, inventions are not made after that manner, and Socrates's history, of which no body entertains any doubt, is not so well attested as that of Christ. Upon the whole, it is removing the difficulty further back, without solving it; for it would be much harder to conceive, that a number of men should have joined together to fabricate this book, than a single person should furnish out the subject to its authors. Jewish writers would never have fallen into that style, or that system of morality; and the gospel hath such strong and such inimitable marks of truth, that the inventor would be more surprising than the hero.[39]

No single passage in Rousseau's writings seems to have appealed to Americans more than this. It was quoted in book, magazine and pamphlet, and in its entirety.[40] Editors seized upon it, reproduced it approvingly, though some expressed bewilderment because it came from Rousseau's pen. One of its uses was to provide ammunition against the deists. The Reverend Uzal Ogden so used the passage in his *Antidote to Deism.* This book had as its purpose the refutation of Paine's *Age of Reason.* The wide and sympathetic response evoked by this passage overshadowed the adverse criticisms of other specific dicta of the Genevan on religion. The latter, indeed, may perhaps be disregarded because they were of disparate and sporadic nature in comparison to the powerful attraction exercised by the celebrated passage.

To recapitulate, one can say that the *Emile* was not much cited on points of general educational theory. Citations of this sort were few, scattered and dissimilar in nature. The same can be said regarding citations of Book V, on female education. My own findings concerning the use of this Book do not bear out the statement above of Mary S. Benson that Rousseau was one whose work on women had "very definite and far-reaching American influence" between 1760 and 1775. I have found one citation on women before 1775 and only a minuscule number after. On the other hand, the author was invoked against deists, and he exerted influence of a sort in support of Christianity. Indeed, I am tempted to conclude that Rousseau's influence was positive in the religious field, negative in the pedagogical. Such findings are of course relative and one gropes in vain for some statistical standard in eighteenth-century America. The writings of other authorities on pedagogy were in circulation. There was Lord Kames, and James Fordyce. Depending on the time and place, Americans could buy "Locke on Education," or "Wollstonecraft on Education," or "Parson's Essays on Education." In fact, Enos Hitchcock, at the beginning of his book on domestic education, declared that "so many treatises have been written, and so many plans laid before the world which promised success; that it [the subject] may be deemed exhausted, and drained of all materials for fabricating a new system, or even for adding to, or improving upon, the old." His book appeared in 1790, about the time, according to H. M. Jones's statement above, that female academies began to proliferate because of the impetus given by Rousseau and the English radical feminists. What was the Genevan's part in all this educational ferment?

There are many signs that his book enjoyed a vogue. Among others, the reader will recall the reference made in 1789 to the "system mongers, who by a superficial perusal of LOCKE, ROUSSEAU, and other benevolent authors, have taken up opinions frequently absurd and grotesque. . . ." And no work of his, as previously indicated, appears to have been advertised more often by American booksellers than the *Emile*. Concerning this vogue, careful attention must be paid to a statement by an authoritative contemporary, Samuel Miller, who, shortly after the turn of the century, wrote: "Among these [treatises on education], perhaps, the celebrated work of Rousseau, under the title of *Emilius*, is most extensively known. This singular production undoubtedly contains some just reasoning, many excellent precepts, and not a few passages of unrivalled eloquence. But it seems to be now generally agreed by sober, reflecting judges, that his system is neither *moral* in its tendency, nor *practicable* in its application."[41] I have already indicated that, according to my findings, the chief influence of the *Emile* was in the field of religion. But let us hear again the words of Miller. Speaking of the extension and improvement of female education, he wrote that "Even the celebrated work of Rousseau has contributed to this end, notwithstanding the visionary and erroneous principles with which it abounds."[42]

8

Other Writings

JOHN MORLEY WROTE THAT "ROUSSEAU'S ECSTATIC vision on the road to Vincennes was the opening of a life of thought and production which only lasted a dozen years, but which in that brief space gave to Europe a new gospel."[1] The meaning is quite clear. The scripture began with the *Discourse on the Arts and Sciences. Emile* closed the canon. And bound in between were the other highly important components of the Rousseauistic evangel, the *Discourse on Inequality, The New Eloisa* and the *Social Contract.* The reader has followed the fortunes of the two Discourses and the three major works. But these were not the only writings in Rousseau's testament. And his period of productivity was by no means confined to a twelve-year span. Accordingly, in this chapter, I wish to direct attention to the knowledge Americans had of other writings and work of the author. I shall present these in the order of the year of their first publication in Europe.

Le Devin du Village

This *Intermède* was staged and printed in Paris in 1753. It was performed, presumably in French, in New York City on October

21, 1790, and repeated on October 26.[2] In 1791, a Philadelphia newspaper carried the announcement of a concert that would include the "Overture Le Devin de Village of Rousseau."[3] The operetta, according to Sonneck, was given twice in French in Charleston, on July 21 and December 6, 1794.[4]

A Dissertation on Political Economy

The essay De l'Economie politique was first printed in the Encyclopédie, V (1755). In translation, it enjoyed the distinction of being an eighteenth-century American imprint. A Dissertation on Political Economy, To which is added, A Treatise on the Social Compact was published in Albany in 1797.[5] More than 200 persons subscribed for the book itself. Philip Freneau also printed serially in 1797 the complete text of the Dissertation on the front pages of his newspaper, the Time-Piece, a triweekly published in New York City.[6]

The only reactions to this essay encountered were those of John Adams. Haraszti, who made a study of his comments, wrote that "Adams was absorbed in the essay, underlining passage after passage. Rousseau's conception of the general will as the source of law for all members of the State especially provoked him."[7] He thought that what Rousseau had to say on inheritance was "worth a volume" but concerning another point made in the essay, Adams exclaimed that "It is amazing that eyes so piercing should be so blind!"[8]

Lettre à d'Alembert sur les spectacles

Originally published in 1758. The New York Society Library's 1773 catalog listed a copy in English.[9] And by 1790, Harvard had copies in both English and French.[10] Joseph Nancrède's anthology, L'Abeille Françoise, published in Boston in 1792, and to which reference has been made, contained extracts from this work.[11] In its issue for May 21, 1808, the *Lady's Weekly Miscellany* printed in translation an extract from d'Alembert's reply to Rousseau.[12]

A Project for Perpetual Peace

This was a reworking by Rousseau of the Abbé de Saint-Pierre's *Projet de paix perpétuelle*.[13] The Genevan's essay was published in both French and English in 1761. Reaction to this essay was unfavorable. James Madison, in an essay on "Universal Peace" (1792) expressed himself in this manner: "Rousseau, the most distinguished of these philanthropists [who have proposed peace projects], has recommended a confederation of sovereigns, under a council of deputies. . . . He was aware neither of the impossibility of executing his pacific plan . . . nor . . . of the tendency of his plan to perpetuate arbitrary power. . . ."[14] He branded the "project of Rousseau" as "preposterous" and "impotent." Joel Barlow, in a letter written from Paris in 1799, "specifically denied the practicability of the 'plan for perpetual peace' originated by Henry IV and 'afterwards embellished with the nervous eloquence of J. J. Rousseau'. . . ."[15] In Boston, the *New-England Quarterly Magazine* reprinted in 1802 a foreign article which referred to the *Project*.[16] *A Project for a Perpetual Peace, by J. J. Rousseau*, was printed in the third volume of *Political Classics*, a work listed in the catalog of the library of Thomas Jefferson.[17] No comment by the third president has been found.

Lettre à Christophe de Beaumont

This *Lettre* is Rousseau's spirited reply to Beaumont, archbishop of Paris, who, in a pastoral letter, condemned the *Emile* for, among other things, its "erroneous, impious, blasphemous and heretical" propositions. The first edition in French appeared in Amsterdam in 1763. The New York Society Library listed an English edition of this *Letter* in its catalog published in 1773.[18] And a French edition was in the Harvard library by 1790.[19]

Pygmalion

This *Scène lyrique,* according to Sénelier, was originally published in Geneva in 1771. It was staged in New York City on November 9, 1790.[20] But it is not clear whether this performance was in French or English. Two forthcoming presentations by French performers were announced to New Yorkers in a newspaper advertisement on March 2, 1796.[21] Actors from Santo Domingo performed the little work in Charleston on February 8, 1794, presumably in French.[22] Between April, 1794 and 1800, it was performed five more times in Charleston, with at least one of the performances in French and two certainly in translation.[23] *Pygmalion* was presented in English to Bostonians in May, 1797.[24]

Lettres à M. de Malesherbes

The four famous letters were first published in Paris in 1779. Joseph Nancrède included these letters in his *Abeille Françoise* (1792).[25]

The Confessions

Part I had originally appeared in 1782 and Part II in 1789. The masterpiece was published in New York in 1796.[26] In the second chapter I have indicated some half-dozen separate advertisements of this work in American newspapers. Both the Library Company of Philadelphia and the New York Society Library had copies on their shelves. Dr. Benjamin Rush read the *Confessions.*[27] Jefferson showed familiarity with the book.[28] And so did Alexander Graydon.[29] William Dunlap, the playwright, noted in his diary in 1798 that he had "Read in Rousseau's Confessions."[30]

Bitter sneers characterized the remarks of Thomas Green Fessenden, who wrote a long poem under the pseudonym of "Christopher Caustic." He ridiculed the Genevan, quoted the autobiography, and noted: "I may perhaps seem unjustifiably harsh in applying the epithet knave to this great modern philosopher. But if the reader will please to consult his confessions he will find a sorry story, which he tells of himself, which is sufficient to justify me in bestowing on him appellations still more severe."[31]

Les Rêveries du Promeneur solitaire

The first edition in French appeared in 1782. A translation, *The Reveries of a Solitary Walker,* was published in New York in 1796.[32] The work seems to have been very infrequently advertised here.[33] The Library Company of Philadelphia had an edition in English.[34]

Considérations sur le Gouvernement de la Pologne

This work was published posthumously in 1782. John Adams cited it in *A Defence of the Constitutions of Government of the United States of America,* first published in part in 1787. In speaking of the scramble of nobles for power, he quoted this statement: "La république de Pologne, a-t-on souvent dit et répété, est composée de trois ordres: l'ordre équestre, le sénat et le roi. J'aimerois mieux dire que la nation polonoise est composée de trois ordres: les nobles, qui sont tout; les bourgeois, qui ne sont rien; et les paysans, qui sont moins que rien."[35]

Lettres élémentaires sur la botanique

Letters on the Elements of Botany . . . Translated into English . . . by T. Martyn were published in London in 1785.[36] Jefferson owned a copy of the 1785 edition, as the catalogue of his second library discloses.[37] The reader's attention has already been called to the listing in 1793 of "Rousseau's *Botany*" in "A

Selected Catalogue of some of the most esteemed Publications in the English Language."[38] And note has been taken of the presence of this work on the shelves of the Library Company of Philadelphia and the South Carolina College Library.[39]

These *opera minora*, which also found their way to the New World, attest the Genevan's amazing productivity, and by their variety they bear further witness to his role as an intermediary of the Enlightenment between France and America. He was truly one of the most versatile of authors. And he continued to write to the very end of life, stopping just short of three months before his death in 1778.

He was also one of Europe's most controversial figures. Rousseau prided himself on being different from the generality of men. And he was. He consecrated his life to the truth as he understood it. He dared to be himself and boldly he revealed to the world the good and the bad about that self. He sought no favor. He was fearless in expressing his ideas. And he had more than one string to his bow. Rousseau would have liked, as someone has suggested, borrowing words from Omar Khayyám, to "shatter Society to bits—and then re-mould it nearer to the heart's desire." Little wonder that he has been a perennial source of curiosity and debate. During his life he knew friend and foe. And in France and Europe, from his day on down, he has had his disciples and his detractors. For Robespierre, he was "the preceptor of mankind." For Samuel Johnson, "Rousseau [was] a rascal who ought to be hunted out of society." Lord Acton, the Cambridge historian, asserted that "Rousseau had produced more effect with his pen than Aristotle, or Cicero, or Saint Augustine, or Saint Thomas Aquinas, or any other man who ever lived."[40] But it would be both easy and tedious to subpoena a host of others who have given contradictory testimony.[41] He has been praised and damned down the years. Indeed, J. Middleton Murry, in a review in the *Monthly Criterion* in 1928, went so far as to call him a "whipping-boy for Jesus. What it is not possible, for reasons of truth, or taste, or expediency, to say about Jesus, can be said, with satisfying violence, about the unfortunate Jean-Jacques." How did he fare with his American readers, separated by an ocean from the prejudices and polemics of Europe? Was ambivalence a characteristic here also? For an answer, let us assay some of the opinions.

9

The Long Ordeal

THE GENEVAN HAS AT ALL TIMES STOOD AT THE
bar of the world's court. Innumerable people have sat in judgment upon him, passed their sentences, and gone their way.
Many, carried away by prejudice against the man, have been
unable to appreciate his writings. Rousseau, as everyone familiar
with the *Confessions* knows, hoped for better understanding at
the Last Judgment.

Here and there in the pages that have preceded, the reader has
noted some rather definite reactions to the author. In this chapter
I shall review these and present others, limiting myself to the
period 1760–1809. I shall try, in so far as possible, to bring into
focus the attitudes toward Rousseau himself, rather than toward
his works. In this way we can follow the deliberations of the
American jurymen and see something of the grounds upon which
they based their opinions. The decisions they came to concerning
the writer himself may possibly throw light on his literary fortunes here. Their verdict upon his writings is reserved for the
final chapter. It is hardly necessary to say that impartial decisions
are not easily arrived at, even under the best of conditions. The

introduction of a political factor, however, can complicate even further the matters at issue. Such appears to have happened in the case of Rousseau. A major political upheaval, the outbreak of the Revolution in France, came to obscure the proceedings.

The French Revolution, someone has said, "drew a red-hot plowshare through the history of America." This observation at once raises questions. Did American attitudes toward Rousseau differ radically before and after the coming of this Revolution? Did the events of the long revolutionary decade prejudice people against him? How impartially was he judged in "the Morning of America?" An examination of the evidence is clearly indicated. Let us then probe first some of the reactions prior to 1789.

"The celebrated Rousseau." That is how James Otis referred to him in 1764. "That restless, fantastical philosopher," wrote Charles Carroll in 1766. "I should not be surprised," said he alluding to the Genevan's stay in England, "at his writing a satire upon the Government on purpose, to draw upon himself a prosecution."[1] Yet, only seven years before, Carroll had thought him one of France's "best authors." In 1776, James Chalmers, another Marylander, spoke of the Genevan, however, as "that sublime reasoner."[2] In 1778, John Adams wrote to his wife that Rousseau "was too virtuous for the age and for Europe. I wish I could not say for another country."[3] Now Haraszti has spoken of Adams's "complicated reactions to the philosopher."[4] The correctness of this observation is to be seen time and time again. Adams could praise and he could defame. A point made in the *Dissertation on Political Economy,* as we saw, made him explode: "It is amazing that eyes so piercing should be so blind."[5] Theophilus Parsons, the Massachusetts jurist, in citing Rousseau authoritatively in the *Essex Result* (1778), referred to him, however, as "a learned foreigner."[6]

Before the French Revolution began, there was, apparently,

very little personal criticism of the author by Americans and only a few minor attacks on his religious views. In 1788, Noah Webster referred to "my *paradoxical* friend Rousseau's advice as to RELIGION."[7] And that same year, William Livingston, in defending Christianity, also used sarcasm in speaking of the Genevan.[8] The search into the evidence for reactions to the man himself, prior to 1789, ends here. They were few indeed in a period covering almost thirty years.

With the outbreak of the Revolution in France, however, reactions in the United States began to multiply. "I know," John Adams wrote in 1790, "that encyclopedists and economists, Diderot and D'Alembert, Voltaire and Rousseau, have contributed to this great event more than Sidney, Locke, or Hoadley, perhaps more than the American revolution; and I own to you, I know not what to make of a republic of thirty million atheists."[9]

The French nation, William Cobbett fulminated, "appears marked out for a dreadful example to mankind. Indeed some such example was necessary to cure the world of the infidel philosophy of Voltaire, Rousseau, Gibbon, Priestley, and the rest of that enlightened tribe."[10] Criticism was to become much more personal and at times vitriolic. The bitter attacks on Rousseau by Cobbett and others were presumably stimulated by the recent publication of several editions of the *Confessions* as well as by the Revolution and its violence in France. Cobbett, Federalist and anti-French, did his utmost to defame the Genevan. Here is a sample: *"Rousseau* is not so well known [as Voltaire]; and, as he was, and still continues to be, the great oracle of the revolutionists, I am persuaded a page or two on his character, and that of his works, will not be lost here; particularly as I have heard both mentioned with applause in this country, by persons apparently of the best intentions."[11] To Cobbett, "applause" indicated a dangerous tendency. He proceeded, therefore, to delineate in most damning fashion unsavory details of the author's career.[12] Then Cobbett added:

> This is a brief sketch of the life of Jean Jacques Rousseau, the oracle of the regenerated French, a thief, a whoremaster, an adulterer, a treacherous friend, an unnatural father, and twice an apostate. . . . His writings, though they have very great literary merit, contain such principles as might be expected from such a man. . . . And his writings are so much the more dangerous, as he winds himself into favour with the unwary, by an eternal cant about *virtue* and *liberty*. He seems to have assumed the mask of virtue for no other purpose than that of propagating, with more certain success, the blackest and most incorrigible vice.[13]

Timothy Dwight attacked the *philosophes* in an address at Yale College. "I shall only add," the Yale president told the students, "that Rousseau (Jean Jacques) is asserted to have been guilty of gross theft, perjury, fornication, and adultery, and of abjuring and assuming, alternately, the Catholic, and the Protestant, religion; neither of which he believed."[14]

Americans also used satires of foreign origin to condemn the man. Here is an example. Signing himself "A Friend to Morality," a writer, in a blistering attack in a periodical, appended "A Prophecy found in an old Manuscript. A Satire on Rousseau," which he had copied from the *Edinburgh Weekly Magazine*. "Its publication in your Repository, will certainly be very proper at this time," he told the editor, "when attempts are made to extenuate the faults, and exonerate the character of one whose writings are calculated to sap the foundations of moral rectitude in the human breast."[15] Another satire of foreign source has been previously discussed. In this satire, printed in a New York state magazine in 1803, Rousseau was called "the genius of contradiction, the scourge of evidence and the inventor of impossible remedies for evils which do not exist." The editor of this magazine, in presenting the satire, lamented that a man of Rousseau's genius "should likewise be the author of sentiments . . . which favour licentiousness and the commission of the worst crimes."[16]

The onslaught, as has been seen, coincided with the revolutionary period. And it did not let up with its close. Thomas Green Fessenden, the American journalist, was one who continued to engage in obloquy. In his long annotated poem, *Democracy Unveiled,* he began the second canto, entitled "Illuminism" in this manner:

> There was a gaunt Genevan priest,
> Mad as our New Lights are at least,
> Much learning had, but no pretence
> To wisdom, or to common sense.

The "New Lights" were the "American Jacobins," those who were "French in their politics." He spoke derisively of Rousseau as "the father of modern Democracy." He was an "odd mixture of heterogenous qualities" and a "knave." The Genevan, said Fessenden contemptuously, was "A very proper person to write political essays, 'Social compacts,' &c. to which mankind are to have recourse for standards in forming a government, and political societies."[17] Fessenden devoted a number of his stanzas on illuminism to Rousseau. He referred to him as the "arch illuminator." He connected the *philosophes* with Adam Weishaupt and the Illuminati, feared a conspiracy to undermine Christianity, overturn society and enthrone reason. Fessenden's apprehensions aside, the belief that Rousseau was one who helped to overthrow the old order in France was rather widespread. John Adams expressed this belief in 1790 and Cobbett in 1796, as their statements above show.[18] From the vantage point of the year 1800, the editor of a religious magazine wrote that "It is unquestionable that he was in the number of those infidels, who prepared the way for that loss of moral principle to which the present convulsions of Europe, may be in part attributed. . . ."[19]

The "Citizen of Geneva" was, indeed, branded variously as an "infidel," an "atheist," a "free thinker" and "an enemy."[20] As deist and *philosophe,* he was a good target. The French Revolution had inflamed the passions of many Americans. It had also opened men's eyes to the dangers of violence. But let us push the inquiry further.

Charles Nisbet had become president of Dickinson College in 1785. In a course on "Moral Philosophy" that he taught there, he told his students that "Rousseau endeavoured to introduce a sentimental philosophy, founded on disinterres [*sic*] friendship, without regard to speculative doctrines, or a future state." And in answer to his own question, "What are we to think of Voltaire, Raynal, Rousseau and Hume, who have appeared as advocates for tolerance?" Nisbet replied: "As all these writers have treated the opinion of all men with injustice and contempt, we cannot suppose that they meant any more than a toleration of their own opinions; tho' not less pernicious to Society than any of those against whom they wrote."[21]

During the Terror, John Adams called Rousseau "a 'Coxcomb,' a 'Fool,' and a 'Satyr,' whose reasoning at times appears to him 'a Mass of Nonsense and Inconsistency.' "[22] Only a few years later Noah Webster would write that "The theories of Helvétius, Rousseau . . . and others, are founded on artificial reasoning, not on the nature of man; not on fact and experience."[23]

Rousseau's was "a mind, inconsistent with itself, and discontented with every present enjoyment," wrote Samuel Harrison Smith. He thought that this mind

> was, without doubt, a great one; it emitted, as copiously as genius or fancy could desire, the sparks of a noble intellect, which dared to disdain the shackles of prejudice, and break the chains of ignorance. But it must be allowed, that in those cases which admitted of personal application, he grossly erred, and generally suffered his strong sense to be overruled by his inexplicable feelings.[24]

In one of the longest articles on the author found in any newspaper, a writer assailed "the *inspired mad-man of Geneva.*" The immediate cause of his annoyance was "a glaring inconsistency in his system of toleration. Towards hereticks, Rousseau appears to be pacific and mild; but against fanaticks, he boldly recommends corporal punishment, and the vigor of the magistrate." This is how he expressed himself in a leading Philadelphia daily:

> Rousseau possessed all the head-strong absurdities of genius. He was a mixture of milk and vinegar, of honey, and of gall, every thing by turns, and nothing long. He has been called a philosopher run mad, an inspired idiot; dull, trifling, impertinent, and disgusting. Yet, it is impossible to deny, that the author of Emilius was a man of genius; now, good, solid, generous, sublime; the next moment vile, contemptible, vain, supercilious, and affected. . . . This sentimental scoundrel is the pagod [idol] of the French revolutionists: his works are in all their hands. This sentiment [he had quoted "the intolerant Philosopher" on fanaticism and the way to deal with it] is the foundation stone, the leading principle, of all their labours; it is thus they would break the sceptre of monarchs by the sword of philosophy. . . . This, Americans, is the toleration you have to expect from a modern philosopher, from a disciple of the French school. If you ever entrust the keeping of your civil and religious liberties to such a man, you deserve justly to suffer all the miseries he can inflict.[25]

In a magazine piece on the "Falsity of the New Fangled Philosophy," a writer said that "So many moral paradoxes and licentious opinions have been published in the world since Rousseau sought distinction by inventing and ingeniously defending absurd doctrines, that one every day meets with new fangled morality recommended by the graces of literature. . . ."[26]

In 1803, Samuel Miller, a Presbyterian minister in New York and a member of the American Philosophical Society, expressed himself as follows:

The character of Rousseau perhaps exhibits the most singular
and humiliating contrasts that were ever displayed in a human
being. Exalted genius and grovelling folly alternately characterized his mind. . . . Oftentimes, when speaking of morality and
religion, one would imagine that sentiments of the most ele-
vated benevolence and piety were habitual to him; but the tenor
of his life, and, indeed, his own *Confessions* demonstrate, that
an unnatural compound of vanity, meanness, and contemptible
self-love, a suspicious, restless temper, bordering on insanity,
and a prostration of every principle and duty, to his own
aggrandisement and gratification, were the real predominant
characteristics of this strange phenomenon in human nature.[27]

Rousseau's character, his way of thinking and his religious
views were objects of numerous attacks. Many belabored the
philosophe.[28] But others praised him highly. One of the latter
was the editor who in 1797 introduced to American readers two
works of Rousseau published here. "It cannot be doubted that
Mr. Rousseau had failings and prejudices," said he, "yet they are
perhaps more than counterbalanced by the solid excellence of
many of his writings. . . ."[29] Another was Elihu Palmer. Rousseau, he wrote, was one of the philosophers of France and
England who "combined their strength in the philanthropic
cause of human improvement; they destroyed error by wholesale,
and swept away the rubbish of ancient superstition [namely,
Christianity], by the irresistible force of a keen and active intel-
ligence."[30] Many others valued various writings of the author.
Epithets such as "great man," "celebrated" and "ingenious" are
coupled with his name as well as epithets of an opprobrious
category. I shall deal with the matter of literary prestige in the
concluding pages of this book.

In the present chapter, the reader can see behind the epithet
the revealing posture of Americans toward the person of Rousseau. Offered here are the findings from a careful examination of
all expressions of opinion having to do primarily with the man

rather than the writer. The evidence speaks for itself. The French Revolution altered profoundly transatlantic thinking. Americans grouped Rousseau with those whom they considered subverters of the established order in France and elsewhere. They stigmatized him as an apostate and an infidel. Before 1789 there was really only John Adams's innuendo that the Genevan "was too virtuous for the age and for Europe. I wish I could not say for another country." After 1789 American attitudes toward him changed radically. Personal criticism increased noticeably in volume and also became much more pointed and acrimonious. The following statement by Samuel Miller sums up fairly well the burden of the criticism: "If the author excelled most other men in genius, he certainly had little claim either to *purity* of character, or real *wisdom.*"[31] In the opinions here reviewed, we see that though many recognized his genius, they attacked his character and questioned his judgment. By some he was accounted erratic and intolerant, foolish and indiscreet. But by others he was praised as a philosopher and philanthropist. Attitudes were ambivalent. Many were attracted by the man's mind but were repulsed by what they had read about him. In their declarations that the Genevan was an unnatural father, an adulterer, and so forth, they obviously drew upon the *Confessions* and other writings of the author, as well as upon satires of foreign origin. He was not spared. Not a few considered his books insidious. Rousseau the man was condemned by the majority of those who expressed an opinion concerning him. In view of the many unfavorable judgments, one can only wonder about the general reception in America of the writings themselves. Our attention turns, then, to the all-important consideration of Rousseau's prestige as author and his literary fortune in the United States.

10

The Final Decision

THE FRENCH REVOLUTION CAST THE LIMELIGHT ON
Rousseau in America. Years before, to be sure, booksellers had
advertised various writings in the colonial press—*The New
Eloisa* as early as 1761, the *Emile* in 1763 and the *Social Contract* as early as 1764. And as far back as 1751, a Virginia
newspaper had carried a mention of the First Discourse. Before
the upheaval, however, Americans had taken little notice of the
author. Mentions and citations of him were few and far between.
But the Revolution attracted attention to him. It made him more
and more conspicuous. Several signs indicate that the real preoccupation with the "Citizen of Geneva" began around 1789. The
increase in the number of newspaper and magazine references to
him and his writings dates from about this time. It was in the
early 1790's that students on the Yale campus jokingly bestowed
on one another the nicknames of "Voltaire," "Rousseau" and
"D'Alembert." And it is perhaps worth recalling that the Library
Company of Philadelphia, in the country's largest city, acquired
an array of Rousseau items in the years between 1789 and 1807.[1]
In the 1790's one also finds books of the author in circulating
libraries and seemingly more anthologies in which passages from

his writings appear. More important is the fact that it was only in the last decade of the century that three American editors, each in a different city, decided to publish one the *Eloisa,* another the *Confessions,* and the third the *Social Contract* and *A Dissertation on Political Economy.* And it was in 1797 that Philip Freneau chose to print the latter work serially on the front pages of the *Time-Piece.* Certain contemporary allusions to some of his books, as we shall see, also afford evidence that the real interest in Rousseau began in the revolutionary period. Most significant of all was the noticeable increase in the volume of comment made on the *philosophe* and his writings that followed the eruption of the volcano.

The reader has had opportunity to examine in the preceding chapter some of the opinions expressed. The attitudes of Americans toward him revealed both attraction and repugnance. Their statements showed concern but by no means indifference. The mass of opinion on Rousseau the man was unfavorable. The *Confessions* had done him great damage. This is one side of the medal. The reader has also seen something of the other side. As an author, he was regarded with favor by many people. It was a signal honor, of course, for him to have had some of his writings published in eighteenth-century America. This was an honor not accorded even Montesquieu. There are numerous indications of esteem. Elihu Palmer, for instance, had spoken in 1804 of "the known reputation of Rousseau, as a writer." And in 1825, Jefferson would make a reference to Rousseau's eminence in America.[2] In these final pages, then, let me direct attention to the evidence of his prestige. This can best be done, I think, if we take a brief look at the reception of each of his major works. The conclusions of the various chapters speak for themselves and need not be repeated in detail in this place. But brief reconsiderations of the fortunes of the writings will throw light on the esteem that Rousseau did or did not enjoy.

The New Eloisa was the most successful of the major works. Jefferson had not hesitated in 1771 to recommend its purchase. It was the delight of numberless people. "What a writer!" exclaimed William Ellery Channing. "Rousseau is the only French author I have ever read, who knows the way to the heart." It appealed to all sorts and conditions of men, to men of such diverse temperaments as John Adams, John Randolph, James Kent, Charles Brockden Brown, Joseph Story, and Samuel Miller. It drew innumerable readers from more humble walks of life. The novel achieved the distinction of "better seller" in 1796.[3] Rousseau the romancer was admired for his talent. Miller said that "among all the French novelists, J. J. Rousseau unquestionably holds the first place as a man of genius." The book had a vogue and, from the evidence, exerted some intangible influence on contemporary American fiction. It also had something of a *succès de scandale.* It came to be regarded here and there as a "pernicious novel" and a book of "bad morals." Even Miller wrote that "Poison lurks in every page." To combat the baleful influence of the Genevan, "whose writings are calculated to sap the foundations of moral rectitude in the human breast," use was made of Charles Bordes' satire of the novel.[4] But so much for tags of immorality. The fact is that, in the decade of the 1790's at least, *The New Eloisa* was a runner-up to best sellers like Hannah Foster's *The Coquette, Gulliver's Travels,* and the plays of Shakespeare.

The role of the *Social Contract* in eighteenth-century American thought has for too long been the almost exclusive center of the scholarly attention paid to Rousseau. No other work by this author has provoked so many assertions concerning its influence or noninfluence. The rapid survey of opinion in the first chapter gives some idea of the extent of this disagreement. Here are the highlights of an investigation in depth as regards this classic and the author's prestige as a political thinker.

American booksellers offered the *Social Contract* to the public only rarely. It was the least advertised of the three major writings, straggling far behind the number of advertisements of *Emile* and *The New Eloisa*. Most of the advertisements of the treatise noted were in the 1790's. When the *Dissertation on Political Economy* and the *Social Contract* were published at Albany in 1797, the editors wrote that "They are indeed here and there in this country to be found on the shelves of such as have with much pains procured them." The evidence tends to bear them out. Books, of course, could be obtained from abroad. And as we saw in the sixth chapter, the *Social Contract* was in the libraries of many prominent Americans. It could also be found occasionally in institutional and circulating libraries. It was used as a textbook at the College of William and Mary.

There were many more references to the book after 1776 than before. Indeed, up to and including 1776, I can only point to some half-dozen citations of the treatise. This fact alone should make one extremely wary of generalizations concerning Rousseau's influence on the Declaration of Independence. In the five-year period preceding the opening of the Federal Convention in 1787, the only citations of the *Social Contract* found were in a pamphlet by Noah Webster. No references to the political classic have been discovered in the Convention year. All the evidence indicates that, in America as also in France itself, the book became better known as the century wore to a close. It attracted more attention and evoked more comment in the decade of the French Revolution than in any other.

Rousseau the political theorist was acclaimed by some, derided by others. Here are samples of attitudes. In 1791, John Quincy Adams, in quoting the *Social Contract,* begged leave to call to his assistance "the authority of Rousseau."[5] In a reference to the book, the writer of a newspaper article published in Philadelphia in 1795 said that "To those humble and timid persons who require the sanction of great names before they can adopt any opinion, I will observe that these were the favorite propositions of Rousseau and Franklin."[6] In 1801, in another newspaper article, a writer asserted that Rousseau's writings "certainly contain many of the principles in theory which have been put into practice by us."[7] This was the year that a student at the College of William and Mary wrote concerning "the mighty fame his treatise on the Social Compact has acquired."[8] In the earliest citation of the work encountered, in 1764, James Otis, the fiery patriot, had referred to "The celebrated Rousseau." And James Chalmers, a Loyalist, had used the same expression and called him "that sublime reasoner" when quoting the *Social Contract* in 1776.[9] Theophilus Parsons, in the *Essex Result* (1778) had spoken of the Genevan as "a learned foreigner" and cited him in language highly suggestive of the political treatise.

In the revolutionary decade and later, the *Social Contract* was also severely criticized. John Adams, Noah Webster, John Quincy Adams, and Thomas Green Fessenden were among the chief detractors. John Quincy Adams, apropos of a point in the *Social Contract,* made the charge in 1791 that it was "neither practicable nor even metaphysically true."[10] In A. O. Hansen's opinion, Webster, whose *Sketches of American Policy* (1785) had been influenced by the treatise on politics, changed his attitude toward the Genevan during the French Revolution.[11] Webster's afterthoughts were that certain ideas in the *Social Contract* were "chimerical" and "too democratic." [12] John Adams who, according to Haraszti, made his notes on the treatise sometime between 1797 and 1801, thought Rousseau's definition of the general will "too mathematical or too witty to be very clear." [13] In 1806, Fessenden spoke of the "absurdities" and the "contradictions" of the *Social Contract,* "a jargon of words without meaning." [14]

What did the *Social Contract* really contribute to the climate of political opinion? According to my findings, little or nothing. Eighteenth-century Americans made some slight but insignificant use of the book. Newspaper editors did not, apparently, reprint extracts from it as they did from the *Spirit of Laws*. It does not seem to have been much quoted in pamphlets of the period. John Witherspoon, who began a course of lectures at Princeton about 1772, did not include Rousseau when he named "Some of the chief writers upon government and politics." The *Social Contract* did not appear in a 1773 catalog of those books more frequently used by Harvard students. In her monograph on *The New England Clergy and the American Revolution,* Alice M. Baldwin showed that there was ample discussion of compact theory by the ministers. But they did not mention Rousseau. No references to the *Social Contract* or its author have been noted in records of the Constitutional Convention of 1787. Neither man nor book was mentioned in *The Federalist* or in the analytical index of the standard edition of the debates on the Constitution in the state ratifying conventions. The Genevan's work on politics was not included in "A Selected Catalogue of some of the most esteemed Publications in the English Language. Proper to form a Social Library," published in Boston near the end of the century.

The fact is that Rousseau's treatise played no significant role in influential contemporary thinking on contractual or any other theory. On the contrary, the political discussions in America directed attention to the *Social Contract*. Many read the book. A few quoted it. But quotation of characteristic passages was extremely rare. Some praised it; others criticized it adversely. Jefferson passed it over in silence. The *Social Contract* exerted no perceptible influence on American political thought. Why was this so?

Noah Webster's comment on this book rings in our ears— "The ideas are too democratic & not just. Experience does not warrant them." Rousseau's ideas were based entirely on theory and those of the American leaders on practical experience. In addition to the wisdom taught by affairs on this continent, these leaders had inherited the practical knowledge gained from long centuries of English trial and error. To the American way of thinking, theories of liberty, equality and government came to the aid of experience, but they had to be made to harmonize with it. One has only to leaf through *The Federalist,* the collection of essays instrumental in securing the adoption of the Constitution, to see the many appeals and references to experience. To Webster and others, though not to everyone, divers principles of the *Social Contract* were visionary. They considered Rousseau impractical.

The *Emile* had a rather wide circulation in the United States. From the survey in the second chapter it appears that no work of the author's was advertised more often by the booksellers than this one. Indeed, it seems to have enjoyed a certain vogue. Franklin, John Adams, Jefferson, Aaron Burr, and Noah Webster were familiar with the classic. And so were many more people, among them schoolmasters, ministers and members of other professions. Jefferson had recommended it in 1771 as a desirable addition to a library. The book, as we have seen, was on the shelves of all sorts of libraries. But paradoxically, it was only occasionally quoted and referred to on pedagogical matters—in print at any rate. The treatise was cited both approvingly and critically. Benjamin Rush mentioned Rousseau favorably in his brief *Thoughts on Female Education* (1787). Enos Hitchcock respected him as an authority on education. Yet Hitchcock, himself the author of an important book on the subject, the *Memoirs of the Bloomsgrove Family* (1790), could also be critical of him. In citing the *Emile* in 1791, the editor of a Philadelphia newspaper referred to its author as "that great man." And in 1807, a Massachusetts minister, quoting the treatise, would speak of the Genevan's "penetration." Americans paid tribute to Rousseau as an authority on pedagogy. But they also esteemed certain other writers in the field. Samuel Miller noted in 1803, however, that Rousseau's work was perhaps the "most extensively known."

As regards educational theory generally, *Emile* does not appear to have been much cited. Its impact on education in eighteenth-century America, according to my findings, was negligible if not nonexistent. Miller believed that the treatise did exert some influence on female education.[15] But from the evidence at hand, I am forced to conclude that Rousseau's influence was negative in the pedagogical field and positive in the religious. I refer to the great success of the passage from the *Profession of Faith of the Savoyard Vicar* found in Book IV of *Emile,* the passage containing the comparison of Socrates and Jesus. This bit of writing moved Americans deeply. It was used to combat deism here. It was extracted and printed more often than any other passage from the author's works. Its vogue and its influence also shed some light on the matter of the author's prestige.

When Elihu Palmer, in 1804, printed the *Profession of Faith of the Savoyard Vicar* almost in its entirety in his magazine, *Prospect,* he declared that the work had had very little circulation in this country. The validity of his assertion is open to question, as the findings regarding the dissemination of *Emile* show. But this is of little moment. What is really significant is that the vogue of the celebrated comparison did not begin until the 1790's, the revolutionary years. The evidence makes this crystal clear. Now in the light of the trivial amount of criticism of Rousseau on specific points of his religious belief, and given the widespread approval of his views as expressed in the famous extract, it seems obvious that some Americans made Rousseau a scapegoat. It appears that he was to some extent a victim of the guilt by association charge. The facts tend to support such a statement as that of Herbert M. Morais that the influence of

French deists here "was greatly exaggerated by Dwight and Payson, who, because of their Federalist affiliations, viewed with alarm the rise of Jeffersonianism which they sought to check by using the French bugaboo."[16]

The fortunes of other writings of the author have been traced in sufficient detail. Only a few reactions to these were noted but some of them throw light on the problem of prestige. John Adams, during the Terror, heaped abuse upon the Genevan for his reasoning in the Second Discourse. But William Hicks had supported his arguments in *The Nature and Extent of Parliamentary Power considered* (1768) by appealing to this same Discourse. The *Dissertation on Political Economy* got into the hands of at least 200 subscribers but the only reactions to it that have come to attention were those of John Adams. What Rousseau had to say in the essay on one subject was "worth a volume" in his opinion but, on another point, Adams was stunned to find him so lacking in discernment. James Madison spoke of Rousseau as "the most distinguished of these philanthropists" to propose projects for peace. But Madison referred to his revision of the Abbé de Saint-Pierre's work, which he called the "project of Rousseau," as "preposterous" and "impotent." [17] The rare opinions on this essay noted were unfavorable. Thomas Green Fessenden made an overt attack on the *Confessions,* called them "a sorry story" and had no hesitancy "in applying the epithet knave to this great modern philosopher." [18] The *Letters on the Elements of Botany* had a certain currency and were included in "A Select Catalogue of some of the most esteemed Publications in the English Language," published by a Harvard librarian in 1793. Indeed, the circulation here of these and other minor writings of the author serves as a further reminder of his importance as an intermediary of the Enlightenment between France and America.

At the beginning of this book I posed three questions which

seem to me basic to any discussion concerning influence: To what degree were the colonists and later Americans acquainted with Rousseau's writings? What did they think of his ideas and theories? What use did they make of them?

Certainly the question of the use to which his writings were put need detain us no longer. With regard to a knowledge of Rousseau, the record shows that colonists and later Americans, in both North and South, had what may be termed a fair acquaintance with his writings. Books of Rousseau were in the libraries of statesmen and clergymen, law professors and judges, teachers, essayists and editors, and men in other walks of life. The array of materials about the author found in various libraries bears further witness to the interest in him. The writings of Voltaire were much more widely advertised and disseminated. As late as 1796, William Cobbett wrote that Rousseau was not as well-known as Voltaire. I have little hesitancy, however, in affirming that, *as a writer,* the Genevan was as well-known here as was Montesquieu, if not more so. But then Rousseau was a man of many books, and Montesquieu was known only for one. In the newspapers themselves, the number of references to Rousseau would not begin to compare with those made to Voltaire. They would not compare too unfavorably, however, with those received by Montesquieu. But the newspapers did not pay the Genevan the compliment, as they did Montesquieu and Voltaire, of reprinting nearly as often copious and lengthy extracts from his writings.

And now to come to grips with the remaining question, the opinion Americans held of his ideas and theories. This question has been answered in detail but in these concluding remarks some general observations are appropriate.

The archenemies of Rousseau were many. Severest among his critics perhaps were Fessenden, Cobbett, and John Adams. They were particularly scornful of some or all of his writings. These men were conservatives. On the other hand, liberals like Philip

Freneau and Elihu Palmer were unsparing in their praise. One is tempted to say that these attitudes were affected by party considerations, although this was not invariably the case. But it is certainly true that Rousseau was caught in the cross fire of American partisan strife. The French Revolution, its ideology and its accompanying violence, had brought very great changes. And Rousseau, as a *philosophe,* rightly or wrongly was held responsible for a share in the catastrophe that befell a continent. Politically, conservatives were frightened of his ideas and theories. They considered him an egalitarian and much too doctrinaire. It is of more than passing interest to recall that it was during the Terror that John Adams, once so enthusiastic about Rousseau, applied to some of his reasoning the phrase, "a Mass of Nonsense and Inconsistency."[19] And it was also during the Revolution that Noah Webster, who had formerly been influenced by the *Social Contract,* spoke of Rousseau's theories as being based on "artificial reasoning, not on the nature of man."[20] Liberals were not afraid of Rousseau's ideas, but on this subject Jefferson remained silent.

The reactions to the ideas contained in *The New Eloisa* and to the pedagogical theories in the *Emile,* summarized above, require no further comment. I should reiterate, however, that many feared the insidious nature of his writings. These two books were doubtless the principal sources of this fear. It is understandable that ministers, editors of religious magazines, and others should protest on behalf of the faithful against the "immorality" of the one and the deism of the other. But such a man as Elihu Palmer, referring to the *Profession of Faith of the Savoyard Vicar* in the latter work, spoke of the "sentiments of virtue" which this writing contained.

Rousseau was his own worst enemy here. As a man he was condemned by the majority of those who expressed an opinion on him. Many obviously had some knowledge of the *Confessions.*

Some of the references to his character, incidentally, shed light on the prestige he enjoyed as author. Cobbett wrote in 1796 that he had heard both his character and his works "mentioned with applause in this country, by persons apparently of the best intentions." In 1797, the publishers of his two works in Albany said that his "failings" were "perhaps more than counterbalanced by the solid excellence of many of his writings." And in a Philadelphia weekly in 1802, one could read that "attempts are made to extenuate the faults, exonerate the character" of Rousseau. Many were the readers who cast stones at the man. It is worth noting, however, that the news items about him appearing in the public press were usually of informative nature, generally favorable, not derogatory.

Rousseau the *writer* was held in high esteem. He had prestige. If there were some who belittled his reasoning, there were others like "Common Sense" who, in 1795, wrote in the *Gazette of the United States* that Rousseau "was himself no inconsiderable Philosopher." But admirer or adversary, almost everyone recognized his genius and literary power. The words of his gospel, whether accepted or not, were heard. They did not fall on stony ground. Here, as elsewhere, he left few readers indifferent. His writings have the power both to attract and to repel. If he was sometimes inconsistent, he was quite often eloquent. This eloquence would provide ammunition to be used against American deists. And this power of language, and the ideas this language clothed, would exercise a charm on many. Among prominent Americans so affected were John Adams, Aaron Burr, Noah Webster, Charles Brockden Brown, John Randolph of Roanoke, Joseph Story, and William Ellery Channing.

It would seem useless to try to arrive at an estimate as to the number of Rousseau's admirers and the number of his adversaries. Such figures would prove nothing. To judge from the number of those who expressed an opinion, I suspect that they were more or less equally divided. But they were not always talking about the same thing. The adversaries, nevertheless, were certainly the most vehement. Much more important than statistics is the nature of his impact. All in all, and excepting the conclusions as regards *The New Eloisa* and the support given religion by the *Emile,* it is obvious that Rousseau had vogue but not influence in eighteenth-century America.

Notes

Preface

1. Harold J. Laski, "A Portrait of Jean Jacques Rousseau," in *The Dangers of Obedience & Other Essays* (New York, 1930), p. 179.

2. I have not, however, seen fit to extend my researches to the French-speaking regions. John F. McDermott's *Private Libraries in Creole Saint Louis* (Baltimore, 1938), for example, discloses the presence of books by Rousseau in some of these libraries between 1764 and 1804.

Chapter 1

1. D. C. Gilman, *James Monroe* (New York, 1898), p. 55.

2. *The Autobiography of Lyman Beecher,* ed. Barbara M. Cross (Cambridge, Mass., 1961), I, 27.

3. *Rousseau and his Era* (London, 1923), I, 3.

4. J. F. Fenton, Jr., *The Theory of the Social Compact and its Influence upon the American Revolution* (n.p., 1891). See his third chapter.

5. E. P. Oberholtzer, *Philadelphia* (Philadelphia, 1912), I, 250.

6. *Liberalism and American Education in the Eighteenth Century* (New York, 1926), pp. 26, 148.

7. *Main Currents in American Thought* (New York, 1927), II, 11.

8. *The Revolutionary Spirit in France and America,* trans. Ramon Guthrie (New York, 1927), p. 79.

9. *Les Philosophes* (New York, 1960), pp. 143–44.

10. *Fundamental Law and the American Revolution, 1760–1776* (New York, 1933), pp. 28–29, 32.

11. *Etat présent des travaux sur J. -J. Rousseau* (New York, 1941), pp. vi–vii n.

12. *Du Contrat social,* ed. C. E. Vaughan (Manchester, 1947), p. 136.

13. *The Growth of American Thought* (New York, 1943), p. 170.

14. Hans Kohn, *The Idea of Nationalism* (New York, 1944), p. 395.

15. Mary S. Benson, *Women in Eighteenth-Century America* (New York, 1935), p. 58.

16. *America and French Culture, 1750–1848* (Chapel Hill, 1927), p. 477.

17. *Cambridge History of American Literature* (New York, 1945), I, 119.

18. J. D. Hart, *The Popular Book* (New York, 1950), p. 33.

19. "Rousseau in Philadelphia," *Magazine of American History,* XII (1884), p. 55.

20. G. P. Fisher, "Jefferson and the Social Compact Theory," *Yale Review,* II (1894), 403–17.

21. *The Critical Period of American History, 1783–1789* (Cambridge, Mass., 1898), p. 66.

22. A. C. McLaughlin, "Social Compact and Constitutional Construction," *American Historical Review,* V (1900), 470.

23. *The Declaration of Independence* (New York, 1904), pp. 197, 198.

24. *The Political Science of John Adams* (New York, 1915), p. 212 n.

25. *The Declaration of Independence* (New York, 1922), p. 27.

26. *The Commonplace Book of Thomas Jefferson* (Baltimore, 1926), p. 44.

27. Clinton Rossiter, *Seedtime of the Republic* (New York, 1953), p. 359.

28. A study by François Jost sheds little if any light on the subject as regards this century, because of insufficient documentation. See his essay, "La Fortune de Rousseau aux Etats-Unis: esquisse d'une étude," *Studies on Voltaire and the Eighteenth Century,* XXV (1963), 899–959. R. R. Palmer, aware of the perplexing nature of the problem, addressed himself to the John Adams-Rousseau relationship. See his article, "Jean-Jacques Rousseau et les Etats-Unis," *Annales historiques de la Révolution française,* XXXIV (1962), 529–40. See also the article of David Williams, "The Influence of Rousseau on Political Opinion, 1760–95," *English Historical Review,* XLVIII (1933), 419–20.

Chapter 2

1. *Maryland Gazette,* Dec. 9, 1762; *Boston Gazette,* Mar. 15, 1762; and *Boston Post-Boy,* Mar. 15, 1762. The advertisement in the Maryland paper, for example, is accompanied by a column and a half of laudatory criticism of the novel taken from *The Critical Review,* in which this translation is praised and the novel compared to Richardson's *Clarissa.*

For other sales announcements of it in Boston, see *Boston Post-Boy,* Sept. 19, 1763; *Boston Gazette,* June 24, 1765; and *Independent Chronicle,* Jan. 20, 1785. Here and elsewhere in the present examination of bookdealers' offerings, an effort has been made to indicate the date of the first appearance only of a given advertisement. Many announcements were repeated over long periods.

2. Theophilus Wreg, *The Virginia Almanack for the Year of our Lord God 1765.*

3. *Federal Intelligencer and Baltimore Daily Gazette,* Dec. 4, 10, 1795. See also a *Catalogue of Books* imported from London . . . via Philadelphia, August, 1808, by Kid and Thomas, Baltimore booksellers.

4. *Boston Gazette,* Dec. 17, 1764.

5. *Columbian Centinel,* May 29, 1793.

6. Ibid., Feb. 27, 1796.

7. Mary E. Loughrey, *France and Rhode Island, 1686–1800* (New York, 1944), p. 107.

8. Wreg.

9. *Boston Gazette,* Jan. 14, 1771; *Independent Chronicle,* Jan. 20, 1785.

10. Loughrey, p. 103.

11. *General Advertiser,* Jan. 21, 1792.

12. *Baltimore Daily Intelligencer,* Oct. 27, 1794; *Federal Intelligencer and Baltimore Daily Gazette,* Dec. 10, 1795. See also *Catalogue of Books* imported from London . . . via New York, September 1808, by Kid and Thomas.

13. J. T. Wheeler, in his article "Booksellers and Circulating Libraries in Colonial Maryland," *Maryland Historical Magazine,* XXXIV (1939), 120, cites an advertisement in the Annapolis *Maryland Gazette,* June 23, 1774 of "An elegant edition of Rousseau's Works, 10 vols. translated from the French." He also notes

[122] the presence of "Rousseau's Whole Works, 10 vols. 60s." in a list of second-hand books purchased by an Annapolis bookseller "from the estate of a deceased clergyman" and offered for sale in the same newspaper on July 20, 1775. I have noted advertisements of the *Works* by a Baltimore dealer in both the *Federal Intelligencer* and the *Maryland Journal* for Oct. 22, 1795.

"Rousseau's Miscellaneous Works" were listed in a *Catalogue of Books to be sold at the Post Office, Williamsburg 176–.*" (Broadside in Rare Book Room, Library of Congress). A Boston bookdealer offered "Rousseau's Miscellaneous Works" in the *Independent Chronicle,* Jan. 13, 1785 and his "Works" (identical item?) in this same paper on Nov. 24, 1785. The "Miscellaneous Works, 5 vols." were advertised by another Boston dealer in the *Columbian Centinel,* Feb. 27, 1796. Also in the *Columbian Centinel* for May 24, 1794, announcement had been made of a forthcoming sale of "A French Library" which included the "Œuvres de Rousseau, 32 vols. in 12mo."

14. For Boston, see *Boston Gazette,* Mar. 29, 1784; *Columbian Centinel,* May 29, 1793 (listed in Dublin bookseller's advertisement to American dealers); ibid., Feb. 27, 1796. For Philadelphia, see *General Advertiser,* June 29, 1791, and for Baltimore, *Baltimore Daily Intelligencer,* Aug. 26, 1794. Most of these advertisements described the edition as being in five volumes, one as having three volumes. The *Confessions,* with *Reveries of the Solitary Walker* had been advertised in the *Providence Gazette* in 1783 and 1784. See Loughrey, p. 103.

15. *Independent Gazetteer,* Nov. 27, 1784.

16. Albert Schinz, "La Librairie française en Amérique au temps de Washington," *Revue d'histoire littéraire de la France,* XXIV (1917), 579. "J. -J. Rousseau" is listed twice and in addition are listed his *Œuvres choisies, Œuvres posthumes,* and "Inégalité, Pygmalion."

17. "Cunning Man, by Mr. Rousseau," offered in *Boston Gazette,* May 11, 1767. This was *Le Devin du Village* in English. *The Cunning-Man,* a translation by Charles Burney, had been published in London in 1766. See *Federal Intelligencer and Baltimore Daily Gazette,* Dec. 10, 1795 for an offering of "Rousseau and Martyn on Botany." Rousseau's "Thoughts, 2 vols." were advertised in Boston in the *Columbian Centinel,* Feb. 27, 1796.

18. "The Importation of French Literature in New York City, 1750–1800," *Studies in Philology,* XXVIII (1931), 782–83. Titles and dates of offerings are as follows: "Les Œuvres de Rousseau" (1772); one notice of the *Emilius* in 1773; three in 1781, another in 1788; "The Whole Works of Rousseau in 11 volumes" (1781); *Works* (1781); "Rousseau" at book auction (1781); *Eloisa* (1788); "Rousseau's Celebrated Confessions" (1798); and "Supplément à la Collection des Œuvres de J. J. Rousseau, 6 tomes" (1798).

On Voltaire's fortune here, see Mary-Margaret H. Barr, *Voltaire in America, 1744–1800* (Baltimore, 1941). Her study is limited to New England and the Middle Atlantic states.

19. "The Importation of French Books in Philadelphia, 1750–1800," *Modern Philology,* XXXII (1934), 163. In the Philadelphia papers, Jones found "some thirteen" advertisements of the *Eloisa,* the first appearing in 1761. There were ten offerings of the *Emilius,* the first in 1763. The *Social Contract* was offered three times, in English in 1764, in French in 1798, and in 1799 (language unspecified). Jones found but one advertisement of the *Confessions,* in 1783. Six advertisements of *Works* or *Œuvres* were noted: in 1784, 1787, 1792, 1797, 1798, and 1799. Advertised also were a "Supplément au contrat social de Rousseau" by Gudin (1792); the "Bigarrures d'un citoyen de Geneva, Rousseau" [in *Freeman's Journal,* Nov. 19, 1783. See note 30 below]; and "Les Pensées" (1788).

20. Jay B. Hubbell, *The South in American Literature, 1607–1900* (Durham, 1954). He writes that "In the *Virginia Gazette's* five longest lists of books Rousseau appears only three times, with 'Rousseau's Eloisa' (twice) and 'Rousseau's Works. 5 Vols.' (once). *Emile* is listed twice in the *Georgia Gazette.* . . . The *Royal Gazette* of Charleston advertised in 1781 'Œuvres de Rousseau, 13 Tom.'" (p. 96 n). Hubbell's findings are excluded from my own survey and calculations.

21. No examination of early nineteenth-century newspaper advertisements has been made for this study. It is of interest, nevertheless, to note the advertisement in the *Norfolk Gazette and Publick Ledger,* May 10, 1805, of the following listings for Rousseau, reproduced here as described: Supplément aux œuvres de; Mélanges de; Pièces & Lettres de; Confessions & Rêveries de; Jugé par Rousseau, Dialogue; Emili par; and Les Politiques de. For source, see

the *Lower Norfolk County Virginia Antiquary*, V (1906), 46. See ibid., II (1897–99), 108 for an offering in the same paper for Nov. 18, 1807 of "Rousseau's Emelius, 2 vol."

22. *Cambridge History of American Literature*, I, 119.

23. Loughrey, p. 106.

24. G. G. Raddin, Jr., *An Early New York Library of Fiction* (New York, 1940).

25. *Eloisa: or, A Series of original Letters. Collected and published by J. J. Rousseau, Citizen of Geneva. Translated from the French. Together with, the Sequel of Julia: or, The New Eloisa. (Found amongst the Author's Papers after his Decease.) First American Edition. Philadelphia: Printed for Samuel Longcope. 1796. 3 vols.* [Charles Evans, *American Bibliography*, XI]

26. *The Confessions of J. J. Rousseau, Citizen of Geneva. Part I.; to which is added, The Reveries of a Solitary Walker; Part II.; To which is added, A New Collection of Letters from the Author; translated from the French.* New York: 1796. 2 vols. [Evans, XI].

27. Albany: Printed and Sold by Barber & Southwick. These writings, the American editors state, were "extracted . . . from a London Translation of Mr. Rousseau's miscellaneous works, printed in 1767."

28. As regards the French edition mentioned in the *Journals of the Continental Congress*, III, 507, supposedly printed in Philadelphia in 1775 "chez John Robert," see note of Christian Gauss in *Annales Jean-Jacques Rousseau*, XI (1916–17), 261–62. In the opinion of Gauss, this was a fictitious and antedated imprint of an edition published in France in 1778. Only one copy of this edition, confiscated by the censorship, was known to him.

For details concerning an edition of the *Contract* in Spanish, purportedly published in Charleston around 1800, see James F. Shearer, "French and Spanish Works, Printed in Charleston, South Carolina," *Papers of the Bibliographical Society of America*, XXXIV (1940), 154 and J. R. Spell, *Rousseau in the Spanish World before 1833* (Austin, 1938), pp. 282 f.

29. *Discurso sobre el orígen y fundamentos de la desigualdad entre los hombres. Por J. J. Rusó, ciudadano de Ginebra. En Charleston. Año MDCCCIII.* See Shearer, p. 149 and Spell, p. 276.

30. *Les Bigarures d'un citoyen de Genève, et ses conseils républicains dédiés aux Américains avec quantités d'Anecdotes amusantes, intéressantes & autres pour servir à terminer l'histoire des Jésuites*

. . . *A Philadelphie de l'Imprimerie du Congrès-Général,* 1776–77. 2 v. See K. R. Gallas, "Un ouvrage faussement attribué à Jean-Jacques Rousseau," *Annales Jean-Jacques Rousseau,* XIII (1920–21), 225–27. See also Eugène E. Rovillain, "Les Bigarures d'un citoyen de Genève (1776–1777)," ibid., XXIII (1934), 163–73. The advertisement in question, according to Rovillain, was printed in the *Freeman's Journal,* Nov. 19, 1783.

31. See Théophile Dufour, *Recherches bibliographiques sur les œuvres imprimées de J.-J. Rousseau* (Paris, 1925), I, 261.

32. *Letters of an Italian Nun and an English Gentleman. Translated from the French of J. J. Rousseau.* The "First Worcester Edition" was printed by Thomas, Son & Thomas at Worcester, Mass. in 1796. This edition included a picture of Rousseau opposite title page. A "Fifth Edition . . . Printed for Mathew Carey" was offered in Philadelphia also in 1796. And in Harrisburgh appeared a "Sixth Edition . . . Printed for Mathew Carey . . . By John Wyeth. 1809."

Chapter 3

1. R. M. Myers, "The Old Dominion Looks to London," *Virginia Magazine of History and Biography,* LIV (1946), 207–208.

2. *France and Rhode Island,* p. 78.

3. See the *Columbian Herald,* Jan. 24, 1785; and the *City Gazette,* Apr. 19, 1791; Feb. 8, 1792; Jan. 7, 1795.

4. The first such reference found by Loughrey was in the *Newport Mercury,* Nov. 21, 1763. See also the *Virginia Gazette,* Mar. 21, 28, Apr. 4, 1766; Aug. 27, 1767; the *Pennsylvania Gazette,* Sept. 20, 1770; the *Massachusetts Centinel,* Aug. 13, Nov. 19, 1788; the *Columbian Centinel,* Nov. 2, 1791; Mar. 31, 1792; the *General Advertiser,* Apr. 25, 1791; Jan. 21, July 21, Sept. 29, Nov. 17, 1792; Dec. 18, 1794; the *National Gazette,* Aug. 8, 1792; the *Federal Intelligencer, and Baltimore Daily Gazette,* Feb. 28, 1795; and the *Gazette of the United States,* Jan. 28, 1795; Aug. 11, 1797; Oct. 15, 1798; Mar. 6, 1801.

5. *Massachusetts Magazine,* V (1793), 452–54.

6. *New-York Magazine,* IV (1793), 707.

7. See Adrian H. Jaffe, *Bibliography of French Literature in American Magazines in the 18th Century* (East Lansing, 1951) and Georges J. Joyaux, "French Thought in American Magazines:

1800–1848." Diss., Michigan State College, 1951. For a few additional findings, see the *Columbian Magazine,* II [Supplement] (1788), 749–50; the *New-York Magazine,* V (1794), 388–92; and the *American Universal Magazine,* I (1797), 96; II (1797), 224. Elihu Palmer quoted the author by name on the title page of the first volume of his magazine, *Prospect; or, View of the Moral World, for the Year 1804.*

8. See Howard C. Rice, *Le Cultivateur américain: Etude sur l'Œuvre de Saint John de Crèvecœur.* In *Bibliothèque de la Revue de littérature comparée,* LXXXVII (1933), 54 and *The Diary of James Gallatin,* ed. Count Gallatin. New ed. (New York, 1920), p. v.

9. See, for example, William Lawrence Brown, *An Essay on the Natural Equality of Men,* 2nd American ed. (Newark, 1802), pp. 10, 67 and 99 nn. He made reference to the First and Second Discourses and the *Contrat social.*

10. Pp. 349–52. For the source, see *La Nouvelle Héloïse,* Lettre LVII.

11. R. B. Davis, *Francis Walker Gilmer* (Richmond, 1939), p. 11 n.

12. Franklin Papers, XVI, 180, American Philosophical Society. The Society also has an undated letter from Mme. Brillon to Franklin asking him to lend her *"le receuil* [sic] *des Romances de J. J. Rousseau."*

13. "The Autobiography of Peter Stephen Du Ponceau," *Pennsylvania Magazine of History and Biography,* LXIII (1939), 459.

14. *The Papers of Thomas Jefferson,* ed. Julian P. Boyd (Princeton, 1955), XI, 269–70, 350.

15. John Bach McMaster, *The Life and Times of Stephen Girard* (Philadelphia, 1918), I, 303. By 1802, the *Rousseau* was launched. Ibid., 405.

16. *Virginia Magazine of History and Biography,* XXIX (1921), 166.

17. G. K. Smart, "Private Libraries in Colonial Virginia," *American Literature,* X (1938), p. 47.

18. J. T. Wheeler, "Reading Interests of Maryland Planters and Merchants 1700–1776," *Maryland Historical Magazine,* XXXVII (1942), 302.

19. M. R. Eiselen, *Franklin's Political Theories* (Garden City, 1928), pp. 4–5.

20. *Papers,* I, 78.

21. C. F. Adams, ed., *Familiar Letters of John Adams and his Wife Abigail Adams, during the Revolution* (New York, 1876), p. 349.

22. "James Madison et la pensée française," *Revue de littérature comparée,* III (1923), 614.

23. J. T. Wheeler, "Booksellers and Circulating Libraries in Colonial Maryland," *Maryland Historical Magazine,* XXXIV (1939), 122.

24. "Narrative of the Prince de Broglie," *Magazine of American History,* I (1877), 378.

25. S. B. Weeks, *Libraries and Literature in North Carolina in the Eighteenth Century.* In *Annual Report of the American Historical Association for the Year 1895* (Washington, 1896), p. 203.

26. V. L. Collins, *President Witherspoon* (Princeton, 1925), II, 208.

27. James Parton, *The Life and Times of Aaron Burr,* enlarged ed. (Boston, 1867), I, 132.

28. Hansen, *Liberalism and American Education in the Eighteenth Century,* p. 203.

29. Lewis Leary, *That Rascal Freneau* (n.p., 1941), pp. 413, 416. According to N. F. Adkins, *Philip Freneau and the Cosmic Enigma* (New York, 1949), p. 20 n., "Ph. Freneau 1786" is inscribed in an odd volume from a 1774 edition in English of Rousseau's works, now in the Princeton University Library.

30. H. H. Clark, "American Literary History and American Literature," in *The Reinterpretation of American Literature,* ed. Norman Foerster (New York, 1959), p. 200.

31. Hester Hastings, *William Ellery Channing and L'Académie des sciences morales et politiques 1870* (Providence, 1959), p. 4.

32. *The Letters of Joseph Dennie 1768–1812,* ed., Laura G. Pedder, *Maine Bulletin,* XXXVIII (1936), xx–xxi.

33. Adrienne Koch and William Peden, eds., *The Selected Writings of John and John Quincy Adams* (New York, 1946), p. 246. See Hachette, II, 166 n.

34. H. A. Garland, *The Life of John Randolph of Roanoke* (New York, 1851), II, 9–10.

35. Catalogue of the library of Chancellor James Kent (1940). Mimeographed copy in the William L. Clements Library.

36. *Life and Letters of Joseph Story,* ed. W. W. Story (Boston, 1851), I, 75–76.

37. *The Works of the Honourable James Wilson* (Philadelphia, 1804), I, 5, 89 n.

38. MS in the Library Company of Philadelphia.

39. *Virginia Magazine of History and Biography,* XXIX (1921), 159–60. See also 266.

40. *Catalogue of the Library of the late Col. William Duane.* This was an auctioneer's catalog, printed in Philadelphia in 1836. There is no way of knowing when Duane (1760–1835) acquired his books.

41. *Catalogue of Books, belonging to the Association Library Company of Philadelphia* (Philadelphia, 1765).

42. *Charter, Laws, and Catalogue of Books, of the Library Company of Philadelphia* (Philadelphia, 1770).

43. *Catalogue of the Books belonging to the Library Company of Philadelphia* (Philadelphia, 1807).

44. *Charter, and Bye-Laws, of the New-York Society Library; with a Catalogue of the Books belonging to the said Library* (New York, 1773).

45. *Catalogue of Books, belonging to the incorporated Charlestown Library Society* (Charlestown, 1770).

46. *Catalogue of Books, given and devised by John Mackenzie Esquire, to the Charlestown Library Society, for the use of the College when erected* (Charlestown, 1772).

47. *Catalogue of Books belonging to the South-Carolina College Library* (Columbia, 1807).

48. Louis Shores, *Origins of the American College Library, 1638–1800* (New York, 1935), p. 94.

49. Josiah Quincy, *The History of Harvard University* (Cambridge, Mass., 1840), II, 529.

50. *Catalogus Bibliothecae Harvardianae* (Boston, 1790).

51. E. J. Bradsher, "A Model American Library of 1793," *Sewanee Review,* XXIV (1916), 462.

52. "Voltaire's works were also found everywhere, and Montesquieu was even more popular; for he was received in the universities, where Rousseau did not appear and where Voltaire entered only by accident." *The Revolutionary Spirit in France and America,* p. 40.

53. *Virginia Magazine of History and Biography,* XXIX (1921), 160.

Chapter 4

1. *Correspondance générale,* ed. Théophile Dufour [and Pierre-Paul Plan], VII (1927), 50–51; Hachette, X, 301–302.

2. *Jean-Jacques Rousseau: Discours sur les Sciences et les Arts.* Edition critique avec une introduction et un commentaire par George R. Havens (New York, 1946).

3. R. M. Myers, "The Old Dominion Looks to London," *Virginia Magazine of History and Biography,* LIV (1946), 207–208.

In 1757, William Smith, Provost of the College and Academy of Philadelphia, attempted to refute the First Discourse. See *Annales Jean-Jacques Rousseau,* XXIV (1935), 267–68.

4. *President Witherspoon,* II, 208.

5. *Old Family Letters: copied from the Originals for Alexander Biddle.* Series A. (Philadelphia, 1892), p. 43. See also his letter to Rush on Sept. 16, 1810, p. 263.

6. An unpublished translation, dated 1756, is now in the Yale University Library. Made by John Farrington of Clapham, near London, it is believed to be the first translation into English. See Richard B. Sewall, "An early manuscript translation of Rousseau's Second *Discourse,*" *Modern Language Notes,* LVII (1942), 271–73. See also Sénelier, p. 66.

7. Loughrey, *France and Rhode Island,* p. 90.

8. See the notes on pp. 5, 6 and 10 of his pamphlet.

9. *Sketches of the Principles of Government* (Rutland, 1793), p. 13. See also p. 31.

10. *The Selected Writings of Benjamin Rush,* ed. Dagobert Runes (New York, 1947), p. 164.

11. *Remarks on Education* (Philadelphia, 1798), p. 27.

12. "John Adams and Rousseau," *Atlantic Monthly,* CLXXXI (1948), 96. The substance of this article is contained in Haraszti's book, *John Adams and the Prophets of Progress* (Cambridge, Mass., 1952), pp. 83–92.

13. John T. Horton, *James Kent* (New York, 1939), pp. 275–76 n.

14. See Henri Roddier, *J.-J. Rousseau en Angleterre au XVIIIe siècle* (Paris, 1950). See also the articles of R. B. Sewall and James H. Warner listed in *A Critical Bibliography of French Literature,* IV (1951), 250–51.

Chapter 5

1. Earl J. Bradsher, *Mathew Carey, Editor, Author and Publisher* (New York, 1912), p. 31.

2. Ibid., p. 120.

3. Emily E. F. Skeel, *Mason Locke Weems* (New York, 1929), II, 182.

4. *Foundations of the Public Library* (Chicago, 1949), p. 154.

5. Hart, *The Popular Book*, pp. 52–53.

6. According to F. G. Black, the *Philadelphia Gazette* proposed in 1796 the publication of "a cheap and elegant pocket edition of select and entertaining novels; or Novelists Pocket Library" which was to include "Julia or the New Eloisa." See his book, *The Epistolary Novel in the late Eighteenth Century* (Eugene, 1940), p. 109 n. To my knowledge, this pocket edition of Rousseau's novel was never printed.

7. The writer is indebted to the article of H. M. Jones, "The Importation of French Books in Philadelphia, 1750–1800," *Modern Philology*, XXXII (1934), 165–66, for calling his attention to the advertisements of Hall and Rivington.

8. "Before any native novelists had appeared, Rousseau's fiction was immensely popular with our readers, his chief novel, translated in England as the *New Eloisa*, becoming between 1761, when it was published, and 1764, when Horace Walpole's *The Castle of Otranto* appeared to supplant it, the most widely read novel in the colonies." *Love and Death in the American Novel* (New York, 1960), p. 82.

9. Willis Steell, *Benjamin Franklin of Paris . . . 1776–1785* (New York, 1928), p. 155.

10. *Catalogue of the Washington Collection in the Boston Athenaeum* (Cambridge, Mass., 1897). Has autograph of "Tim. Pickering" on the bastard title-page.

11. *William and Mary College Quarterly Historical Magazine*, XI (1902–1903), 27.

12. Loughrey, *France and Rhode Island*, p. 102.

13. *Memoirs and Letters of James Kent*, ed. William Kent (Boston, 1898), p. 27.

14. W. C. Bruce, *John Randolph of Roanoke, 1773–1833* (New York, 1922), I, 61.

15. *Life and Letters of Joseph Story,* I, 75–76.

16. Ibid., p. 79.

17. *Memoir of William Ellery Channing,* 6th ed. (Boston, 1854),
I, 102.

18. Gilbert Chinard, "Notes de John Adams sur Voltaire et Rousseau," *Modern Language Notes,* XLVI (1931), 26–31. He owned an
edition in French, in four volumes, published in Neufchâtel in 1764.
See also Haraszti, *John Adams and the Prophets of Progress,* pp.
96–98.

19. *Catalogue of the Library of the late Rev. J. S. Buckminster*
(Boston, 1812).

20. Pp. 169–70.

21. II (1791), 438–40.

22. See André Ruplinger, *Charles Bordes* (Lyons, 1915), pp.
58–60.

23. Skeel, III, 22–23.

24. *The Spirit of the Farmer's Museum* (Walpole, N. H., 1801),
pp. 284–85.

25. *A Brief Retrospect of the Eighteenth Century* (New York,
1803), II, 163.

26. Pp. 78–97. For the notes, see pp. 97–108.

27. *That Rascal Freneau,* p. 148.

28. See the edition of Freneau's *Poems written between the years
1768 & 1794* (Monmouth, New Jersey, 1795), p. 123.

29. III (1797), 216.

30. *Studies in Philology,* XXVIII (1931), 783.

31. "Sensibility in the Eighteenth-Century American Novel,"
Studies in Philology, XXIV (1927), 393.

32. *The Sentimental Novel in America, 1789–1860* (Durham,
N.C., 1940), p. 75 n.

33. *The Epistolary Novel in the Late Eighteenth Century* (Eugene, 1940), pp. 73–74 n.

34. Lulu R. Wiley, *The Sources and Influence of the Novels of
Charles Brockden Brown* (New York, 1950).

35. D. L. Clark, *Charles Brockden Brown* (New York? 1923), p.
21.

36. Harry R. Warfel, *Charles Brockden Brown* (Gainesville,
1949), p. 63.

37. *The Rhapsodist and Other Uncollected Writings by Charles*

Brockden Brown, ed. Harry R. Warfel (New York, 1943), p. 71.
   38. *Golden Multitudes* (New York, 1947), pp. 305, 316–17.

Chapter 6

   1. Quoted from his edition of Rousseau's *Du Contrat social* (Manchester, 1947), p. liii.
   2. See Sénelier.
   3. Pp. 3–5. The editors added a few footnotes themselves to the *Social Compact,* which they were careful to label as their own. See pp. 87 and 203. According to W. O. Clough, *Our long Heritage* (Minneapolis, 1955), p. 196, the Albany edition followed the text of the translation published in London in 1764. In 1797 also, the *American Universal Magazine,* Philadelphia, extracted and reprinted chapter X ["Of the People"] from the Second Book of the *Social Contract.* See the magazine, IV, 61–64.
   4. Loughrey, *France and Rhode Island,* p. 90.
   5. Hubbell, *The South in American Literature,* p. 96.
   6. Raddin, *An Early New York Library of Fiction,* pp. 18, 21.
   7. *Catalogus librorum in Bibliotheca Cantabrigiensi selectus* (Boston, 1773).
   8. *Virginia Magazine of History and Biography,* XXIX (1921), 159–60.
   9. *Early History of the University of Virginia, as contained in the Letters of Thomas Jefferson and Joseph C. Cabell,* ed. N. F. Cabell (Richmond, 1856), p. 47. Jefferson recommended "The Review of Montesquieu" [Destutt de Tracy's *A Commentary and Review of Montesquieu's Spirit of Laws* (Philadelphia, 1811)] and this was the text-book the president adopted. See pp. 53 and 69, *Early History.*
   10. *Catalogue of the Washington Collection,* p. 523.
   11. *Diary and Autobiography of John Adams,* eds. L. H. Butterfield *et al.* (Cambridge, Mass., 1961), I, 255.
   12. Haraszti, *John Adams and the Prophets of Progress,* p. 95. See pp. 95–96 for comments of Adams on Rousseau's treatise.
   13. *Catalogue of the Library of Thomas Jefferson,* ed. E. M. Sowerby (Washington, 1952), III, 16. In third volume of *Political Classics,* published in London, 1794–95. Not initialed by Jefferson.

This is the catalog of Jefferson's second library. On his various libraries, see also R. G. Adams, *Three Americanists* (Philadelphia, 1939), pp. 73–74.

14. *Works,* ed. Charles Francis Adams (Boston, 1850–56), III, 454–55. See also *Diary and Autobiography,* I, 254.

15. *Observations on the Act of Parliament commonly called the Boston Port-Bill; with Thoughts on Civil Society and Standing Armies* (Boston, 1774).

16. Theodore Roosevelt, *Gouverneur Morris* (Boston and New York, 1898), p. 27.

17. See p. iii of the edition prepared by Harry R. Warfel and published in 1937.

18. *The Papers of Alexander Hamilton,* eds. H. C. Syrett and J. E. Cooke (New York, 1962), V, 150.

19. *The Works of the Honourable James Wilson,* I, 89 n. See also his reference to "The eloquent Rousseau" on p. 5.

20. *General Advertiser,* July 2, 1791.

21. Ibid., July 20, 1791.

22. Ibid., July 28, 1791.

23. *Observations on the Emigration of Dr. Joseph Priestly* [*sic*], 4th ed. (Philadelphia, 1796), p. 38.

24. See Victor C. Miller, *Joel Barlow: Revolutionist, London, 1791–92* (Hamburg, 1932), pp. 60, 70. And Leon Howard, in *The Connecticut Wits* (Chicago, 1943), p. 287, writes that ". . . although he did not mention Rousseau by name, the *Advice* [Barlow's *Advice to the Privileged Orders,* the first part of which was published in London in 1792] contains a sufficient number of occasional parallels to the *Social Contract* to indicate that Barlow had read that book, even though he did not accept its argument."

25. Leary, *That Rascal Freneau,* p. 278.

26. *Democracy Unveiled, or, Tyranny stripped of the Garb of Patriotism,* 3rd ed. (New York, 1806). I, 41–42. The quotations from the *Contract* were from Book I, chapters 1 and 6; II, chapters 3 and 5. See pp. 39–41 of Fessenden's book.

27. *Memoirs of a Life* (Edinburgh, 1822), p. 263. See also pp. 420–21. The memoirs extend to about 1807.

28. *Lectures on Moral Philosophy,* ed. V. L. Collins (Princeton, 1912), p. 70.

29. *The Records of the Federal Convention of 1787,* 3 vols. (New Haven, 1927).

30. *The Debates in the several State Conventions, on the Adoption of the Federal Constitution, as recommended by the General Convention at Philadelphia in 1787,* ed. Jonathan Elliot, 2nd ed. (Washington, 1836).

31. Horace E. Scudder, *Noah Webster* (New York, 1882), p. 119.

32. Kingsley Martin, *French Liberal Thought in the Eighteenth Century* (Boston, 1929), p. 218.

33. *The Declaration of Independence,* p. 27.

34. "Jefferson and the Freedom of the Human Spirit," *Ethics,* LIII (1943), 238.

35. *Puritanism and Democracy* (New York, 1944), p. 126.

36. 2nd ed., revised (Ann Arbor, 1957), p. 87.

37. *The Commonplace Book of Thomas Jefferson,* p. 44.

38. Ibid., p. 63.

39. *The Literary Bible of Thomas Jefferson* (Baltimore, 1928).

40. *Thomas Jefferson,* pp. 84–85. See also Chinard's *La Déclaration des Droits de l'Homme et du Citoyen et ses antécédents américains* (Washington, 1945), pp. 24 ff., and Herbert L. Ganter, "Jefferson's 'Pursuit of Happiness' and Some Forgotten Men," *William and Mary Quarterly,* 2nd ser., XVI (1936), 422–34, 558–85.

41. For Rousseau's views, see André Lichtenberger, *Le socialisme au XVIII° siècle* (Paris, 1895) and for Jefferson's, Richard Schlatter, *Private Property: The History of an Idea* (New Brunswick, 1951).

42. In 1825, Jefferson, then Rector of the University of Virginia, wrote to William Hilliard, Boston bookdealer, complaining that the latter had sent to the University library "Œuvres de Rousseau. J. B. . . . altho' in the catalogue I did not specify Jean Jaques [*sic*] Rousseau, yet his eminence over the other would entitle him to be understood of preference." Elizabeth Cometti, *Jefferson's Ideas on a University Library* (Charlottesville, 1950), p. 36.

43. See, among others, the introductions to the following editions of Rousseau's book: *Du Contrat Social,* ed. C. E. Vaughan (Manchester, 1947); *The Social Contract,* ed. Charles Frankel (New York, 1957). See also Sir Ernest Barker's Introduction to *Social Contract; Essays by Locke, Hume and Rousseau* (New York, 1948) and R. R. Palmer, *The Age of the Democratic Revolution: A*

Political History of Europe and America, 1760–1800 (Princeton, 1959), I, 120–27.

44. J. W. Gough, *The Social Contract: A Critical Study of its Development,* 2nd ed. (Oxford, 1957), pp. 229–43.

45. Bernard Faÿ, "La Langue française à Harvard" in *Harvard et la France* (Paris, 1936), p. 170 n.

46. Francis G. Wilson, *The American Political Mind* (New York, 1949), p. 44.

47. See Max Farrand, *The Fathers of the Constitution* (New Haven, 1921), pp. 39–40; Baldwin, *The New England Clergy and the American Revolution,* p. 24; and Gough, p. 86.

48. See Merle Curti, "The Great Mr. Locke: America's Philosopher," *Huntington Library Bulletin,* No. 11, April, 1937.

49. Gough, p. 89.

50. See, for example, Jefferson's letter in 1783 to Edmund Randolph, *Papers,* VI, 247–48. For Hamilton, see Number 21 of *The Federalist,* and *Papers,* III, 535, 549; V, 294.

51. Haraszti, *John Adams and the Prophets of Progress,* p. 95.

52. Chinard, *Thomas Jefferson,* p. 85.

53. In the opinion of R. R. Palmer, a phrase in the preamble to the Massachusetts Constitution of 1780, written by John Adams, was possibly "deposited" by Rousseau in Adams's mind. This phrase, "The body politic is formed by a voluntary association of individuals. It is a social compact. . . ." The entire passage in which these words occur, according to Palmer, "suggests" chapter 6 of the first Book of the *Social Contract. The Age of the Democratic Revolution,* I, 223–24.

54. *Les Origines intellectuelles de la Révolution française, 1715–1787,* 5th ed. (Paris, 1954) ". . . il est impossible d'en discerner l'influence sur les origines mêmes de la Révolution. . . . et qu'on ne réunirait pas dix témoignages de lecteurs qui, avant 1789, aient reçu de l'œuvre une impression forte." [p. 96]. In his well-known article, "Les Enseignements des bibliothèques privées (1750–1780)," *Revue d'Histoire littéraire de la France,* XVII (1910), a study of the contents of 500 libraries, Mornet found only one copy of the *Contrat social.* See also Joan McDonald, *Rousseau and the French Revolution 1762–1791* (London, 1965), pp. 43–50.

55. See, in addition to McDonald, Gordon H. McNeil, "The Anti-Revolutionary Rousseau," *American Historical Review,* LVIII

(1953), 808–23 and Phyllis S. Robinove, "The Reputation of the Philosophes in France, 1789–1799." Diss., Columbia Univ., 1955, p. 134.

56. Cf. Palmer, I, 119.

Chapter 7

1. L.-J. Courtois, *Chronologie critique de la vie et des œuvres de Jean-Jacques Rousseau.* In *Annales Jean-Jacques Rousseau,* XV (1923). Reprinted separately in Geneva in 1924.

2. Ibid.

3. For short expositions in English, see William Boyd, *Emile for Today* (London, 1956); George R. Havens, *The Age of Ideas* (New York, 1955); and Ernest Hunter Wright, *The Meaning of Rousseau* (London, 1929).

4. See, among others, the article of Maurice Debesse, "L'Influence pédagogique de l'*Emile* depuis deux siècles. Ses formes, son évolution," in *Jean-Jacques Rousseau et son œuvre, Problèmes et Recherches* (Paris, 1964), pp. 205–17.

5. *L'Abeille Françoise ou Nouveau Recueil de Morceaux brillans, des auteurs François les plus célèbres . . . à l'usage de L'Université de Cambridge* (Boston, 1792).

6. "Un 'Rousseauiste' en Amérique (*L'Abeille Française,* de Joseph Nancrède)," *Modern Language Notes,* XXXV (1920), 13.

7. See, for example, pp. 177–79, 182–83, 206–207, 208–10, 262–65 and 266–67. The source of each passage is to be found, respectively, in Hachette II, 165–67, 138–39, 184–85, 103–105, 49–51, and 46.

8. Henry Jones Ford, *Alexander Hamilton* (New York, 1925), p. 22.

9. Loughrey, p. 102.

10. *The Writings of Benjamin Franklin,* ed. A. H. Smyth (New York, 1907), IX, 334–35. Hachette II, 11 ff.

11. *Essays, Literary, Moral & Philosophical* (Philadelphia, 1798), pp. 82–83. Id., *Columbian Magazine,* April, 1790. Cf. Hachette II, 60–62. In a "Sermon on Exercise" [1772] he also approved of Rousseau's saying that "Women only should follow those mechanical arts which require a sedentary life." [Rush's words]. See *The Selected Writings of Benjamin Rush,* p. 363.

12. *Catalogue of the John Adams Library in the Public Library of the City of Boston* (Boston, 1917).

13. *Old Family Letters.* Series A, p. 57.

14. Nathan Schachner, *Aaron Burr* (New York, 1937).

15. David Ramsay, *Memoirs of the Life of Martha Laurens Ramsay* (Philadelphia, 1811). "She was well acquainted with the plans of Rousseau, and other modern reformers, who are for discarding the rod and substituting confinement, and other visionary projects in its place; but considered them all as inferior in efficacy, to the prudent use of the rod. . . ." p. 31.

16. *Life and Letters of Joseph Story,* I, 75–76. A quotation from the fifth Book of *Emile* appears on the title page of *An Oration, delivered at Concord, on the Anniversary of American Independence, July 4th, 1801. By Samuel P. P. Fay.* Cambridge, 1801. His quotation does not concern female education.

17. P. 90.

18. *General Advertiser,* June 7, 1791. Reprinted in the *Gazette of the United States,* Aug. 21, 1795. See Hachette II, 165 ff.

19. *General Advertiser,* Oct. 10, 1792. Reprinted "From the Universal Asylum." In a letter from Allison to Benjamin Rush dated July 2, 1792. Cf. Hachette II, 45.

20. *Women in Eighteenth-Century America,* p. 58.

21. *America and French Culture,* p. 476.

22. Heading: "A Speech addressed from a Father to his Daughter. From the French of M. Rousseau." Hachette II, 371–73.

23. Pp. 38–39. See also p. 41. For above, cf. Hachette II, 329.

24. *New York Magazine,* n.s. II (1797), 406. Cf. Hachette II, 345. Article reprinted from a foreign publication, the *Monthly Magazine,* for March, 1797.

25. Pp. 17, 34.

26. *A Discourse . . . at the Annual Meeting of the Salem Female Charitable Society* (Salem, 1807), p. 16. Hachette II, 360.

27. VII (1808), 269.

28. *Memoirs of the Bloomsgrove Family. In a Series of Letters . . . containing Sentiments on a Mode of domestic Education, suited to . . . Society, Government, and Manners, in the United States of America. . . .*

29. Alexander Cowie, *The Rise of the American Novel* (New York, 1948), p. 17.

30. Benson, p. 155.

31. See I, 52, 82, 175–76, 236, 285–86; II, 43–47 and 207–209.

32. Concerning this last view, Benjamin Rush in his *Thoughts upon Female Education* was of like mind with Hitchcock. So was Noah Webster, writing under the pseudonym of "Belzebub" in the *American Magazine,* I (1788), 86.

33. *Travels; in New-England and New-York* (New Haven, 1822), IV, 366.

34. *American Museum or Repository,* IV (1788), 441.

35. *The Bloody Buoy,* 2nd ed. (Philadelphia, 1796), p. 237.

36. Jan. 4, 1803. According to the note, the "Profession" was originally published in Amsterdam in 1763.

37. *The Autobiography and Ministerial Life of the Rev. John Johnston, D.D.,* ed. James Carnahan (New York, 1856), p. 91.

38. I, 171–72. See Numbers 22–50 inclusive (May 5 through Nov. 17, 1804). Extracts appeared in every one of these numbers except one, that for Aug. 18. The magazine also printed on April 21 of the same year "A letter of Rousseau to his Bookseller at the Hague." The letter concerns the "Savoyard's Creed, inserted in my Emilius. . . ." [pp. 156–57].

39. See Hachette, II, 280–81.

40. See Uzal Ogden, *Antidote to Deism. The Deist Unmasked* (Newark, 1795), I, 29–31 [Ogden said that he quoted the passage from a pamphlet, *The Age of Infidelity: in Answer to Thomas Paine's Age of Reason. By a Layman.* This was written by Thomas Williams. Originally published in London, it was reprinted in 1794 in Boston, Salem, Worcester, New York and Philadelphia. The passage in the Philadelphia reprint is found on pp. 15–17]; Michel Martel, *Martel's Elements* (New York, 1797), II, 608–10 [in French]; *American Universal Magazine,* II (1797), 348–50; *Connecticut Evangelical Magazine,* I (1800), 71–72; *Weekly Visitant,* I (1806), 149–50; and *Moral and Religious Cabinet,* I (1808), 268–69. The lines in the passage comparing the deaths of Socrates and Jesus were also quoted by Joseph Priestley in his pamphlet, *Socrates and Jesus Compared* (Philadelphia, 1803), p. 43, and by Eliphalet Nott, president of Union College, in *An Address, delivered to the Candidates for the Baccalaureate, in Union College . . . July 29, 1807* (Albany, 1807), p. 23.

41. *Brief Retrospect,* II, 271.

42. Ibid., II, 284.

Chapter 8

1. *Rousseau* (London, 1915), I, 136.
2. O. G. Sonneck, *Early Opera in America* (New York, 1915), pp. 199–200. Without being specific, H. M. Jones wrote that "in 1791 a company of French comedians and singers gave vaudeville and operas in New York—works by Grétry and Rousseau being among the number. . . ." *America and French Culture,* p. 338. H. C. Lahee, *Annals of Music in America* (Boston, 1922), p. 11, also affirmed that between 1790 and 1800, *Le Devin du Village* and *Pygmalion* (see below) were performed by a company of French comedians in New Orleans, Charleston, Baltimore, Philadelphia and New York City.
3. *General Advertiser,* Mar. 18, 1791.
4. P. 206. Edward D. Seeber also noted two performances of the operetta in Charleston between April, 1794 and 1800 but found it difficult from newspaper advertisements to say whether in French or English. See his article "The French Theatre in Charleston in the Eighteenth Century," *South Carolina Historical and Genealogical Magazine,* XLII (1941), 6. See chap. 2, n. 17, for a bookseller's advertisement in 1767 of an English translation of *Le Devin du Village.*
5. See chap. 2, n. 27.
6. In the issues from August 28 through September 13.
7. *John Adams and the Prophets of Progress,* p. 93. It would be of interest to know when Adams made his comments. Haraszti indicates only that Adams read the essay in a 1764 edition of the *Œuvres de Rousseau,* which was in his library.
8. Ibid., p. 95
9. Chap. 3, n. 44
10. Chap. 3, n. 50.
11. See pp. 213–18 and 241–46.
12. VII, 59–60. For this as well as some other findings in periodicals, I am indebted to Georges J. Joyaux, "French Thought in American Magazines: 1800–1848."
13. C. E. Vaughan, *The Political Writings of Jean Jacques Rousseau* (Cambridge, Eng., 1915), I, 359 ff.
14. *Letters and Other Writings of James Madison* (Philadelphia, 1865), IV, 470. Rousseau also wrote a *Jugement* on the Abbé de

Saint-Pierre's *Projet,* though this was not known in the eighteenth century. In it, Rousseau said: "Qu'on ne dise donc point que, si son système n'a pas été adopté, c'est qu'il n'étoit pas bon; qu'on dise au contraire qu'il étoit trop bon pour être adopté." In the *Confessions,* Rousseau commented that the Abbé's projects were useful, but impractical, "par l'idée dont l'auteur n'a jamais pu sortir, que les hommes se conduisoient par leurs lumières plutôt que par leurs passions." See George R. Havens, *Voltaire's Marginalia on the Pages of Rousseau* (Columbus, The Ohio State University, 1933), pp. 37–38.

15. Howard, *The Connecticut Wits,* pp. 304–305.

16. The Abbé de Saint-Pierre's "project of 'An Universal Peace,' by the infelicity of his style, could find no readers; a philanthropist as singular, but more eloquent, the celebrated Rousseau, embellished the neglected labour, enabled us to read the performance, and perceive its humane imbecility." Number II, p. 253.

17. See chap. 6, n. 13.

18. Chap. 3, n. 44.

19. Chap. 3, n. 50.

20. Sonneck, *Early Opera in America,* p. 200.

21. Arnold Whitridge, "Brillat-Savarin in America," *Franco-American Review,* I (1936), 8. Sonneck cites a performance in English in New York on Mar. 13, 1796. See Table B, following p. 90.

22. Lewis P. Waldo, *The French Drama in America in the Eighteenth Century* (Baltimore, 1942), p. 194.

23. Seeber, pp. 6–7.

24. Waldo, p. xiv.

25. Pp. 128–49. According to Schinz, "Un 'Rousseauiste' en Amérique," p. 14, the text of the four letters reprinted was almost complete.

26. See chap. 2, n. 26.

27. *The Autobiography of Benjamin Rush,* ed. G. W. Corner (Princeton, 1948), p. 91.

28. *The Writings of Thomas Jefferson,* Definitive ed. (Washington, 1905), XIV, 469.

29. *Memoirs of a Life,* p. 50.

30. *Diary of William Dunlap,* ed. Dorothy C. Barck (New York, 1930), I, 349.

31. *Democracy Unveiled,* 3rd ed., I, 35. See also ibid., pp. 17, 21–22, 32 n., 33–37.

32. See chap. 2, n. 26.

33. Chap. 2, nn. 14 and 21.

34. Chap. 3, n. 43.

35. *Works,* IV, 366–67 n. Hachette V, 252–53.

36. I have not examined this first edition but in the seventh edition (London, 1807), p. vii, Martyn stated that he translated the *Letters* from the *Collection complète des Œuvres de J.-J. Rousseau,* published in Geneva in 1782.

37. *Catalogue of the Library of Thomas Jefferson,* I, 482.

38. Chap. 3, n. 51.

39. Chap. 3, nn. 43 and 47.

40. *Letters of Lord Acton to Mary, Daughter of the Right Hon. W. E. Gladstone,* ed. Herbert W. Paul (London, 1904), p. xii.

41. Cf. Lichtenberger, *Le socialisme au XVIIIe siècle,* pp. 128–30.

Chapter 9

1. Joseph Gurn, *Charles Carroll of Carrollton, 1737–1832* (New York, 1932), p. 32.

2. *Plain Truth,* p. 2.

3. *Familiar Letters of John Adams and his Wife Abigail Adams,* p. 349.

4. *John Adams and the Prophets of Progress,* p. 81.

5. Chap. 8, n. 8.

6. *Result of the Convention of Delegates . . . in the County of Essex, who were Deputed to take into Consideration the Constitution and form of Government proposed by the Convention of the State of Massachusetts-Bay* (Newbury-Port, 1778), p. 10.

7. Chap. 7, n. 32.

8. Chap. 7, n. 34.

9. *Works,* IX, 563–64.

10. *Observations on the Emigration of Dr. Joseph Priestley,* 4th ed., p. 47.

11. *The Bloody Buoy,* 2nd ed., p. 232. Concerning Voltaire, see Barr, *Voltaire in America.*

12. *The Bloody Buoy,* pp. 232–36.

13. Ibid., pp. 236–37. In an article in the *Gazette of the United*

States, April 29, 1796, a writer transcribed Cobbett's strictures from *The Bloody Buoy.*

14. *The Nature, and Danger, of Infidel Philosophy . . . two Discourses, addressed to the Candidates for the Baccalaureate in Yale College* (New Haven, 1798), p. 47.

15. *Philadelphia Repository, and Weekly Register,* II (1802), 297. Charles Bordes was the author of this satire, "Prédiction tirée d'un vieux manuscrit." See chap. 5, n. 22. Cobbett, in the second edition of *The Bloody Buoy,* had also printed a part of this satire in a note to page 238.

16. Chap. 7, n. 36.

17. *Democracy Unveiled,* 3rd ed., I, 32 n. See also pp. 17, 33–35. Cf. chap. 8, n. 31.

18. See also the review by a Hartford writer of a pamphlet of Edmund Burke's in the *General Advertiser,* Apr. 15, 1791; Noah Webster, *The Revolution in France* (New York, 1794), p. 18; and the poem signed by "An American" in the *Gazette of the United States,* Nov. 17, 1798. Webster was not uncomplimentary here to Rousseau. But in his *Ten Letters to Dr. Joseph Priestly* [*sic*], *in Answer to his Letters to the Inhabitants of Northumberland* (New Haven, 1800), p. 21, he condemned him and others for theories which led to the blood bath of the French Revolution.

19. *Connecticut Evangelical Magazine,* I (1800), 72.

20. Cf. John Foster, *Infidelity exposed, and Christianity recommended* [a sermon] (Cambridge, Mass., 1802), pp. 21, 33; *Port Folio,* new ser., V (1808), 76; and the *Moral and Religious Cabinet,* I (1808), 268–69.

21. See pp. 3 and 86 of the MS of these lectures in the Library Company of Philadelphia.

22. Chap. 4, n. 12.

23. *Ten Letters to Dr. Joseph Priestley, p.* 21. According to A. O. Hansen, Webster's "change of view from his earlier position when he believed in the doctrines of Rousseau, began to take form in his reactions to the French Revolution about 1793." *Liberalism and American Education in the Eighteenth Century, p.* 206.

24. *Remarks on Education,* p. 32.

25. *Gazette of the United States,* July 25, 1800.

26. *New England Quarterly Magazine,* number I (1802), 93.

27. *Brief Retrospect,* II, 163 n. See also p. 271. Cf. chap. 5, n. 25.

Years afterward, according to a biographer, Burr would "say of Rousseau that he was well named 'a self-torturing egotist.'" Burr "had little relish, in his later years, for the French authors who had pleased him so much in his youth." Parton, *The Life and Times of Aaron Burr,* II, 275.

28. In this chapter, I have taken care to present only American judgments. Purposely excluded from consideration are the attacks on Rousseau by foreigners whose writings circulated or were reprinted in the United States. Cf. Joseph Priestley, *An Answer to Mr. Paine's Age of Reason* (Northumberland Town, 1794), pp. 36–37; the Rev. John Bennett, *Letters to a Young Lady on a Variety of Useful and Interesting Subjects* (New York, 1796), II, 40; Robert Hall, *Modern Infidelity considered with Respect to its Influence on Society* [sermon] (Charlestown, Mass., 1801), p. 32. Bennett's remarks had already been quoted in the *American Museum,* XII (1792), 19. Both the *Monthly Anthology,* April, 1806, pp. 190–91, and the *Literary Tablet,* May 28, 1806, reprinted an article on the "Character of Rousseau" from Robert Fellowes' *A Picture of Christian Philosophy.* Here one could read that "The exposure of his children, by whatever sophistry it may be excused, is an indelible blot on his humanity; and invalidates all his pretensions to philanthropy." Priestley, in the pages above, also referred to the abandonment of his children.

29. Chap. 6, n. 3.

30. *Principles of Nature,* 2nd ed. (New York, 1802), p. 184. For statements of others who praised Rousseau's role in the Enlightenment, see John I. Johnson, *Reflections on Political Society* (New York, 1797), p. 15; "Americanus" in the *Gazette of the United States,* Aug. 11, 1797 (reprinted from the *Virginia Gazette*); and James Ogilvie, *Cursory Reflexions on Government, Philosophy and Education* (Alexandria, 1802), p. 11.

31. *Brief Retrospect,* II, 271.

Chapter 10

1. Chap. 3, n. 43.
2. Chap. 6, n. 42.
3. Chap. 5, n. 38.
4. Chap. 5, nn. 20, 21; chap. 9, n. 15.
5. Chap. 6, n. 22.

6. *Aurora General Advertiser,* Oct. 16, 1795. Article by "Casca," reprinted from the *Petersburg Intelligencer.*

7. *Aurora General Advertiser,* Jan. 26, 1801.

8. Chap. 6, n. 8. Philip Freneau had referred to the book in 1797 as "one of the most popular works of the celebrated J. J. Rousseau."

9. *Plain Truth,* p. 2. Hachette III, 327.

10. Chap. 6, n. 20.

11. Chap. 9, n. 23.

12. Chap. 6, n. 17.

13. *John Adams and the Prophets of Progress,* p. 95. Years later, in 1813, Adams would write to Jefferson as follows: "I have never read Reasoning more absurd, Sophistry more gross, in proof of the Athanasian Creed, or Transubstantiation, than the subtle labours of Helvetius and Rousseau to demonstrate the Natural Equality of Mankind. Jus cuique; the golden rule; do as you would be done by; is all the Equality that can be supported or defended by reason, or reconciled to common Sense." *The Adams-Jefferson Letters,* ed. L. J. Cappon (Chapel Hill, 1959), II, 355.

14. Chap. 6, n. 26.

15. Chap. 7, n. 42.

16. *Deism in Eighteenth Century America* (New York, 1934), p. 148.

17. Chap. 8, n. 14.

18. Chap. 8, n. 31.

19. Chap. 4, n. 12.

20. Chap. 9, n. 23.

Bibliography

I. *ROUSSEAU MATERIAL CITED IN THIS BOOK*

a. EDITIONS OF HIS WRITINGS

Confessions . . . . *to which is added, The Reveries of a Solitary Walker* . . . . *To which is added, A New Collection of Letters from the Author* . . . . 2 vols. New York, 1796.

Correspondance générale, ed. Théophile Dufour [and Pierre-Paul Plan]. 20 vols. Paris: A. Colin, 1924–34.

Discours sur les Sciences et les Arts. Edition critique par George R. Havens. New York: The Modern Language Association of America, 1946.

Dissertation on Political Economy: To which is added, A Treatise on the Social Compact; or, the Principles of Politic Law. Albany: Barber & Southwick, 1797.

Du Contrat social, ed. Charles Edwyn Vaughan. Manchester: At the University Press, 1947.

Eloisa: or, A Series of original Letters . . . . *Together with, the Sequel of Julia: or, The New Eloisa* . . . . *First American Edition,* 3 vols. Philadelphia: Printed for Samuel Longcope, 1796.

Œuvres complètes de J. J. Rousseau. 13 vols. in 7. Paris: Hachette, 1909–14.

"Rousseau, J. J. the Gospel of Reason." In Charles Pigott's *Political Curiosities.* London. 1794–95; Philadelphia: Printed for Richard Lee [1796?].

Social Contract: Essays by Locke, Hume and Rousseau, ed. Sir Ernest Barker, New York: Oxford University Press, 1948.

Social Contract, The, ed. Charles Frankel, New York: Hafner Publishing Company, 1957.

b. Books and Articles on Rousseau

Annales de la Société Jean-Jacques Rousseau. 36 vols. Geneva: Jullien, 1905—.

Boyd, William. *Emile for Today: The Emile of Jean-Jacques Rousseau.* London: Heinemann, 1956.

Chinard, Gilbert. "Notes de John Adams sur Voltaire et Rousseau," *Modern Language Notes,* XLVI (1931).

Courtois, L.-J. *Chronologie critique de la vie et des œuvres de Jean-Jacques Rousseau.* Geneva: Jullien, 1924.

Critical Bibliography of French Literature, A, ed. D. C. Cabeen and others. 4 vols. and a Supplement to Volume IV: The Eighteenth Century. Syracuse: Syracuse University Press, 1947—.

Debesse, Maurice. "L'Influence pédagogique de l'*Emile* depuis deux siècles. Ses formes, son évolution." In *Jean-Jacques Rousseau et son œuvre, Problèmes et Recherches.* Paris: Klincksieck, 1964.

Dufour, Théophile. *Recherches bibliographiques sur les œuvres imprimées de J.-J. Rousseau.* 2 vols. Paris: Giraud-Badin, 1925.

Ghibaudi, Silvia Rota. *La Fortuna di Rousseau in Italia, 1750–1815. Turin:* Edizioni Giappichelli, 1961.

Haraszti, Zoltán. "John Adams and Rousseau," *The Atlantic Monthly,* CLXXXI (1948).

———. *John Adams and the Prophets of Progress.* Cambridge, Mass.: Harvard University Press, 1952.

Havens, George R. *The Age of Ideas: from Reaction to Revolution in eighteenth-century France.* New York: Henry Holt & Company, 1955.

————. *Voltaire's Marginalia on the Pages of Rousseau.* Columbus: The Ohio State University, 1933.

Jost, F. "La Fortune de Rousseau aux Etats-Unis: esquisse d'une étude," *Studies on Voltaire and the Eighteenth Century,* XXV (1963).

Laski, Harold J. "A Portrait of Jean Jacques Rousseau," in his *The Dangers of Obedience & Other Essays.* New York: Harper & Brothers, 1930.

McDonald, Joan. *Rousseau and the French Revolution 1762–1791.* London: University of London, Athlone Press, 1965.

McNeil, Gordon H. "The Anti-Revolutionary Rousseau," *American Historical Review,* LVIII (1953).

Morley, John Morley, *viscount. Rousseau.* 2 vols. London: Macmillan & Company, Limited, 1915.

————. *Rousseau and his Era.* 2 vols. London: Macmillan & Company, Limited, 1923.

Palmer, R. R. "Jean-Jacques Rousseau et les Etats-Unis," *Annales historiques de la Révolution française,* XXXIV (1962).

Roddier, Henri. *J.-J. Rousseau en Angleterre au XVIII° siècle,* Paris: Boivin, 1950.

Rosenthal, Lewis. "Rousseau in Philadelphia," *Magazine of American History,* XII (1884).

Schinz, Albert. *Etat présent des travaux sur J.-J. Rousseau.* New York: Modern Language Association of America, 1941.

Sénelier, Jean. *Bibliographie générale des Œuvres de J.-J. Rousseau.* Paris: Presses Universitaires de France, 1950.

Sewall, R. B. "An early manuscript translation of Rousseau's Second *Discourse,*" *Modern Language Notes,* LVII (1942).

Spell, J. R. *Rousseau in the Spanish World before 1833.* Austin: University of Texas Press, 1938.

Vaughan, Charles Edwyn. *The Political Writings of Jean-Jacques Rousseau.* 2 vols. Cambridge, Eng.: University Press, 1915.

Williams, David. "The Influence of Rousseau on Political Opin-
ion, 1760–95," *English Historical Review*, XLVIII (1933).
Wright, Ernest Hunter. *The Meaning of Rousseau.* London:
Oxford University Press, 1929.

II. CONTEMPORARY SOURCES

a. Documents and Manuscripts

Brillon, Mme. Undated letter of, to Benjamin Franklin. American Philosophical Society.
Elliot, Jonathan, ed. *The Debates in the several State Conven-
tions, on the Adoption of the Federal Constitution, as
recommended by the General Convention at Philadelphia
in 1787.* 2nd ed. 4 vols. Washington: Printed for the
Editor, 1836.
Farrand, Max, ed. *The Records of the Federal Convention of
1787.* 3 vols. New Haven: Yale University Press, 1927.
*Federalist, The. A Collection of Essays written in favour of the
New Constitution as agreed upon by the Federal Conven-
tion, September 17, 1787.* 1st ed. 2 vols. New York: J. and
A. M'Lean, 1788.
Franklin Papers, XVI, 180. American Philosophical Society.
Journals of the Continental Congress. 34 vols. Washington:
Government Printing Office, 1904–37.
Nisbet, Charles. Lectures on Moral Philosophy. Library Com-
pany of Philadelphia.

b. Printed Books

Adams, C. F., ed. *Familiar Letters of John Adams and his Wife
Abigail Adams, during the Revolution.* New York: Hurd
& Houghton, 1876.
Adams, John. *Diary and Autobiography,* eds. L. H. Butterfield
et al. 4 vols. Cambridge, Mass.: Belknap Press of Harvard
University Press, 1961.
———. *Works,* ed. Charles Francis Adams. 10 vols. Boston:
Little, Brown & Company, 1850–56.

Anon. *The Art of Courting*. Newburyport: William Barrett, 1795.

Bailyn, Bernard. *Pamphlets of the American Revolution, 1750–1776*. 1 vol. Cambridge, Mass.: Belknap Press of Harvard University Press, 1965—.

Beccaria, Cesare Bonesana, *marchese* di. *An Essay on Crimes and Punishments*. Philadelphia: R. Bell, 1778.

Beecher, Lyman. *Autobiography*, ed. Barbara M. Cross. 2 vols. Cambridge, Mass.: Belknap Press of Harvard University Press, 1961.

Bell, Robert. *Illuminations for legislators, and for sentimentalists*. Philadelphia: Robert Bell, 1784.

Bennett, John. *Letters to a Young Lady on a Variety of Useful and Interesting Subjects*. 2 vols. New York: Printed by John Buel, for E. Duyckinck & Company, 1796.

Bentley, William. *A Discourse . . . at the Annual Meeting of the Salem Female Charitable Society*. Salem: Pool & Palfray, 1807.

Broglie, Prince de. "Narrative of the . . . ," trans. E. W. Balch, *Magazine of American History*, I (1877).

Brown, Charles Brockden. *The Rhapsodist and Other Uncollected Writings*, ed. Harry R. Warfel. New York: Scholars' Facsimiles & Reprints, 1943.

Brown, W. L. *An Essay on the Natural Equality of Man*, 2nd American ed. Newark: John Wallis, 1802.

Cappon, Lester J. *The Adams-Jefferson Letters*. 2 vols. Chapel Hill: University of North Carolina Press, 1959.

Carey, Mathew. *The School of Wisdom: or, American Monitor*. Philadelphia: Printed for Mathew Carey, 1800.

[Chalmers, James]. *Plain Truth; addressed to the Inhabitants of America, containing Remarks on a late Pamphlet entitled Common Sense*. Philadelphia: R. Bell, 1776.

Chinard, Gilbert, ed. *The Commonplace Book of Thomas Jefferson: A Repertory of his Ideas on Government*. Baltimore: The Johns Hopkins Press, 1926.

Chipman, Nathaniel. *Sketches of the Principles of Government.* Rutland: Printed for the Author, 1793.

Clarke, John. *Letters to a Student in the University of Cambridge, Massachusetts.* Boston: Samuel Hall, 1796.

Cobbett, William. *The Bloody Buoy, thrown out as a Warning to the political Pilots of America.* Philadelphia: Printed for Benjamin Davies, 1796. A 2nd ed. was also published in this city in the same year.

———. *Observations on the Emigration of Dr. Joseph Priestly* [*sic*]. 4th ed. Philadelphia, 1796.

Dennie, Joseph. *Letters . . . 1768–1812,* ed. Laura G. Pedder, *The Maine Bulletin,* XXXVIII (1936).

Destutt de Tracy. *A Commentary and Review of Montesquieu's Spirit of Laws.* Philadelphia: William Duane, 1811.

Dunlap, William. *Diary,* ed. Dorothy C. Barck. 3 vols. New York: Printed for the New York Historical Society, 1930.

Du Ponceau, Peter Stephen. "The Autobiography of . . . ," *Pennsylvania Magazine of History and Biography,* LXIII (1939).

Dwight, Timothy. *The Nature, and Danger, of Infidel Philosophy . . . two Discourses, addressed to the Candidates for the Baccalaureate in Yale College.* New Haven: George Bunce, 1798.

———. *Travels; in New-England and New-York.* 4 vols. New Haven: T. Dwight, 1821–22.

Fay, Samuel P. P. *An Oration, delivered at Concord, on the Anniversary of American Independence, July 4th, 1801.* Cambridge, Mass.: William Hilliard, 1801.

Fessenden, Thomas Green. *Democracy Unveiled, or, Tyranny stripped of the Garb of Patriotism.* 3rd ed. 2 vols. in 1. New York: Printed for I. Riley & Company, 1806.

Foster, John. *Infidelity exposed, and Christianity recommended.* Cambridge, Mass.: William Hilliard, 1802.

Franklin, Benjamin. *Writings,* ed. A. H. Smyth. 10 vols. New York: The Macmillan Company, 1905–1907.

Freneau, Philip. *Poems written between the years 1768 & 1794.* Monmouth, N.J.: Printed at the Press of the Author, 1795.

Gallatin, James. *Diary,* ed. Count Gallatin, new ed. New York: C. Scribner's Sons, 1920.

[Graydon, Alexander]. *Memoirs of a Life, chiefly passed in Pennsylvania, within the last sixty years.* Edinburgh: W. Blackwood, 1822.

Hall, Robert. *Modern Infidelity considered with Respect to its Influence on Society.* Charlestown, Mass.: Samuel Etheridge, 1801.

Hamilton, Alexander. *Papers,* eds. H. C. Syrett and J. E. Cooke. 11 vols. New York: Columbia University Press, 1961—.

[Hicks, William]. *The Nature and Extent of Parliamentary Power considered.* Philadelphia: W. and T. Bradford, 1768.

Hitchcock, Enos. *Memoirs of the Bloomsgrove Family. In a Series of Letters . . . containing Sentiments on a Mode of domestic Education, suited to . . . Society, Government, and Manners, in the United States of America . . . .* 2 vols. Boston: Printed at Thomas and Andrews, 1790.

Jefferson, Thomas. *Literary Bible,* ed. Gilbert Chinard. Baltimore: The Johns Hopkins Press, 1928.

―――. *Papers,* ed. Julian P. Boyd. 17 vols. Princeton: Princeton University Press, 1950—.

―――. *Writings.* Definitive ed. 20 vols. in 10. Washington: Issued under the auspices of the Thomas Jefferson Memorial Association of the United States, 1905.

Johnson, John I. *Reflections on Political Society.* New York: Freneau & Menut, 1797.

Johnston, John. *Autobiography and Ministerial Life,* ed. James Carnahan. New York: M. W. Dodd, 1856.

Kent, James. *Memoirs and Letters,* ed. William Kent. Boston: Little, Brown, & Company, 1898.

Koch, Adrienne and William Peden, eds. *The Selected Writings of John and John Quincy Adams.* New York: A. A. Knopf, 1946.

Mackenzie, Henry. *The Man of Feeling . . . With the senti-*

mental Sailor. A Poem, originating from Rousseau's Eloisa.
Philadelphia: Robert Bell, 1782.

Madison, James. *Letters and Other Writings.* 4 vols. Philadelphia: J. B. Lippincott & Company, 1865.

Martel, Michel. *Martel's Elements.* 2 vols. New York, 1796–97.

Miller, Samuel. *A Brief Retrospect of the Eighteenth Century.* 2 vols. New York: T. and J. Swords, 1803.

Nancrède, Joseph. *L'Abeille Françoise ou Nouveau Recueil de Morceaux brillans, des auteurs François les plus célèbres . . . à l'usage de L'Université de Cambridge.* Boston: Belknap & Young, 1792.

Nott, Eliphalet. *An Address, delivered to the Candidates for the Baccalaureate, in Union College . . . July 29, 1807.* Albany: Webster & Skinner, 1807.

Ogden, Uzal. *Antidote to Deism. The Deist Unmasked.* 2 vols. Newark: John Woods, 1795.

Ogilvie, James. *Cursory Reflexions on Government, Philosophy and Education.* Alexandria: J. & J. D. Westcott, 1802.

Old Family Letters: copied from the Originals for Alexander Biddle. Series A. Philadelphia: Press of J. B. Lippincott Company, 1892.

Otis, James. *The Rights of the British Colonies Asserted and Proved.* Boston: Edes & Gill, 1764.

Palmer, Elihu. *Principles of Nature,* 2nd ed. New York, 1802.

Parsons, Theophilus. *Result of the Convention of Delegates . . . in the County of Essex, who were Deputed to take into Consideration the Constitution and form of Government proposed by the Convention of the State of Massachusetts-Bay.* Newbury–Port: John Mycall, 1778.

Polwhele, Richard. *The Unsex'd Females.* New York: Republished by Wm. Cobbett, 1800.

Priestley, Joseph. *An Answer to Mr. Paine's Age of Reason.* Northumberland Town, 1794.

———. *Socrates and Jesus Compared.* Philadelphia: P. Byrne, 1803.

Quincy, Josiah, Jr. *Observations on the Act of Parliament commonly called the Boston Port-Bill; with Thoughts on Civil*

Society and Standing Armies. Boston: Printed for and sold by Edes & Gill, 1774.

Rush, Benjamin. *Autobiography*, ed. G. W. Corner. Princeton: Princeton University Press, 1948.

———. *Essays, Literary, Moral & Philosophical*. Philadelphia: Thomas & Samuel F. Bradford, 1798.

———. *Selected Writings*, ed. D. Runes. New York: Philosophical Library, 1947.

———. *Thoughts upon Female Education, accommodated to the present State of Society, Manners, and Government, in the United States of America*. Philadelphia: Prichard & Hall, 1787.

Smith, Samuel Harrison. *Remarks on Education* . . . . Philadelphia: Printed for John Ormrod, 1798.

Story, Joseph. *Life and Letters*, ed. W. W. Story. 2 vols. Boston: C. C. Little & J. Brown, 1851.

Webster, Noah. *Sketches of American Policy* (1785), ed. Harry R. Warfel. New York: Scholars' Facsimiles and Reprints, 1937.

———. *Ten Letters to Dr. Joseph Priestly* [*sic*], *in Answer to his Letters to the Inhabitants of Northumberland*. New Haven: Read & Morse, 1800.

———. *The Revolution in France*. New York: G. Bunce and Company, 1794.

Williams, Thomas. *The Age of Infidelity: in Answer to Thomas Paine's Age of Reason*. Philadelphia: Reprinted for Stephen C. Ustick, 1794.

Wilson, James. *Works*, ed. Bird Wilson. 3 vols. Philadelphia: Bronson & Chauncey, 1804.

Witherspoon, John. *Lectures on Moral Philosophy*, ed. V. L. Collins. Princeton: Princeton University Press, 1912.

c. Newspapers and Magazines

American [Baltimore]. Daily. May 14–Dec. 12, 1799; June 6–Dec. 31, 1800; Jan. 1–Mar. 7, 1801. Maryland Historical Society.

American Magazine [New York]. Nos. 1–12 (Dec., 1787–Nov., 1788).

American Magazine and Monthly Chronicle for the British Colonies [Philadelphia]. I (Oct., 1757–Oct., 1758).

American Monthly Review; or, Literary Journal [Philadelphia]. I–III (Jan.–Dec., 1795).

American Museum or Repository [Philadelphia]. 12 vols. (Jan., 1787–Dec., 1792).

American Universal Magazine [Philadelphia]. I–IV (Jan. 2, 1797–Mar. 7, 1798).

Aurora General Advertiser [Philadelphia]. Daily. Nov. 8, 1794–Dec. 31, 1797; Jan. 2–Feb. 13, Aug. 2, Sept. 7, Nov. 1–16, 23, 1798; Jan. 15, 1799; Sept. 4, Oct. 21, 1800; Jan. 1–Mar. 7, 1801. Complete as indicated. Philadelphia libraries, Library of Congress and the Maryland Historical Society.

Balance and Columbian Repository. Jan. 4, 1803.

Baltimore Daily Intelligencer. Jan. 1–Oct. 29, 1794. Maryland Historical Society and Peabody Library.

Boston Gazette or Country Journal. Weekly. 1760–87. Library of Congress.

Boston Magazine. Oct., 1783–Sept., 1784; Sept.–Oct., 1786.

Boston Post-Boy. Mar. 15, 1762; Sept. 19, 1763.

City Gazette [Charleston]. Apr. 19, 1791; Feb. 8, 1792; Jan. 7, 1795.

Columbian Centinel [Boston]. Semiweekly. June 16, 1790–Mar. 18, 1801. Library of Congress.

Columbian Herald [Charleston]. Jan. 24, 1785.

Columbian Magazine; or monthly miscellany [Philadelphia]. I–IV (Sept., 1786–June, 1790).

Connecticut Evangelical Magazine [Hartford]. I–VII (1800–1806/07); n.s., I–II (1808–1809).

Federal Gazette and Baltimore Daily Advertiser. Jan. 1, 1796–Mar. 1, 1797. Peabody Library.

Federal Intelligencer and Baltimore Daily Gazette. Oct. 30–Dec. 30, 1794; Jan. 1, 1795–Jan. 1, 1796. Maryland Historical Society and Peabody Library.

Gazette of the State of South Carolina [Charleston]. June 13, 1785.

Gazette of the United States. Semiweekly and daily. [Established at New York, Apr. 15, 1789. Continued at Philadelphia, Nov. 3, 1790. Became a daily with issue of Dec. 11, 1793]. Complete through issue of Mar. 7, 1801, except the following: Jan. 25, 27, Aug. 28–Dec. 31, 1797; July 12–31, Aug. 18–30, 1798. Library of Congress, Maryland Historical Society and Philadelphia libraries.

General Advertiser, and Political, Commercial, Agricultural and Literary Journal [Philadelphia]. Daily. Oct. 1, 1790–Nov. 7, 1794. Complete. Library of Congress and Philadelphia libraries.

General Magazine, and Impartial Review [Baltimore]. June and July, 1798.

Independent Gazetteer [Philadelphia]. Nov. 27, 1784.

Independent Chronicle [Boston]. Weekly. 1785. Many issues examined for this year.

Lady's Weekly Miscellany, VII (1808).

Literary Tablet. May 28, 1806.

Maryland Gazette [Annapolis]. Weekly. Jan. 3, 1760–Dec. 30, 1773. Complete except for issue of Jan. 2, 1772. Library of Congress, Maryland Historical Society and Maryland State Library.

Maryland Journal and Baltimore Advertiser. Weekly, semiweekly, and triweekly. Aug. 20, 1773–July 1, 1797. Library of Congress and Maryland Historical Society. Between the two libraries files are almost complete.

Massachusetts Centinel and the Republican Journal [Boston]. Semiweekly. Mar. 24, 1784–June 12, 1790. Library of Congress.

Massachusetts Magazine, or Monthly Museum, V (1793).

Monthly Anthology, and Boston Review, I–V (Nov., 1803–Dec., 1808).

Moral and Religious Cabinet, I (1808).

National Gazette. [Philadelphia]. Semiweekly. Oct. 31, 1791–

Oct. 26, 1793. Complete. Library of Congress and Ridgway branch of the Library Company of Philadelphia.

National Magazine; or, A political, historical, biographical, and literary repository [Richmond]. 3 vols. (June 1, 1799–Dec. 22, 1800).

New-England Quarterly Magazine, nos. 1 and 2 (1802).

New Hampshire Magazine [Concord]. July, 1793.

New Haven Gazette, and the Connecticut Magazine. I (Feb. 16, 1786–Feb. 5, 1787); II (Feb. 22–Dec. 27, 1787).

New-Jersey Magazine, and monthly Advertiser [New Brunswick]. Dec., 1786 and Jan., 1787.

New-York Magazine, or Literary Repository [New York]. I–VI (Jan., 1790–Dec., 1795); n.s., I–II (Jan., 1796–Dec. 1797).

Pennsylvania Gazette [Philadelphia]. Jan. 28, Feb. 4, 1762; Sept. 20, 1770.

Pennsylvania Magazine: or, American Monthly Museum [Philadelphia]. I–II (Jan., 1775–July, 1776).

Pennsylvania Packet [Philadelphia]. Oct. 1, 1782.

Philadelphia Repository, and Weekly Register, II (1802).

Port Folio [Philadelphia]. N.s., I–V (1806–1808).

Prospect; or, View of the Moral World [New York]. I (1804).

Royal American Magazine, or Universal repository of instruction and amusement [Boston]. I and II, nos. 1–3 (Jan., 1774–Mar., 1775).

South Carolina Gazette [Charleston]. Supplement, Nov. 1, 1773.

South-Carolina Weekly Museum [Charleston?]. I (Jan.–July, 1797). Library of Congress. Fair file.

Spirit of the Farmer's Museum, and Lay Preacher's Gazette. Walpole, N. H.: D. & T. Carlisle, for Thomas & Thomas, 1801.

Time-Piece; and Literary Companion [New York]. Triweekly. Aug. 28–Sept. 13, Dec. 8, 1797.

Virginia Gazette [Williamsburg]. Weekly. Jan. 16, 1761; Feb. 12, 1762; 1766–67, good; 1775, complete; 1776–77, good; 1778, very poor; 1779–80, good. Library of Congress.

————. Rind's [Williamsburg]. Changed from weekly to semiweekly with issue of Dec. 6, 1775. 1766–68, not very many. Library of Congress.

Weekly Visitant, I (1806).

Worcester Magazine. 4 vols. (Mar., 1786–Mar., 1788). Library of Congress. Fair file.

d. CATALOGS

Catalogue of Books, belonging to the Association Library Company of Philadelphia. Philadelphia: William Bradford, 1765.

Catalogue of Books, belonging to the incorporated Charlestown Library Society. Charlestown: Robert Wells, 1770.

Catalogue of Books belonging to the South-Carolina College Library. Columbia: Daniel & J. J. Faust, 1807.

Catalogue of Books, given and devised by John Mackenzie Esquire, to the Charlestown Library Society, for the use of the College when erected. Charlestown: Robert Wells, 1772.

Catalogue of Books imported from London . . . via New York, Sept., 1808, by Kid & Thomas, Baltimore booksellers.

Catalogue of Books imported from London . . . via Philadelphia, Aug., 1808, by Kid & Thomas.

Catalogue of Books to be sold at the Post Office. Williamsburg 176–. Broadside in Rare Book Room, Library of Congress.

Catalogue of the Books belonging to the Library Company of Philadelphia. Philadelphia: Bartram & Reynolds, 1807.

Catalogue of the John Adams Library in the Public Library of the City of Boston. Boston: Published by the Trustees, 1917.

Catalogue of the Library of the late Rev. J. S. Buckminster. Boston: John Eliot, Jr., 1812.

Catalogue of the Library of the late Col. William Duane. Philadelphia, 1836.

Catalogue of the Library of Thomas Jefferson, ed. Emily Millicent Sowerby. 5 vols. Washington: Library of Congress, 1952–59.

Catalogue of the library of Chancellor James Kent (1940). Mimeographed copy in the William L. Clements Library.

Catalogue of the Washington Collection in the Boston Athe-naeum. Cambridge, Mass.: University Press, 1897.

Catalogus Bibliothecae Harvardianae. Boston: Thomas & John Fleet, 1790.

Catalogus librorum in Bibliotheca Cantabrigiensi selectus. Boston: Edes & Gill, 1773.

Charter, and Bye-Laws, of the New-York Society Library; with a Catalogue of the Books belonging to the said Library. New York: H. Gaine, 1773.

Charter, Laws, and Catalogue of Books, of the Library Company of Philadelphia. Philadelphia: Joseph Crukshank, 1770.

Harris, Thaddeus M. *A Selected Catalogue of some of the most esteemed Publications in the English Language. Proper to form a Social Library.* Boston: Thomas & Andrews, 1793.

Wreg, Theophilus. *The Virginia Almanack for the Year of our Lord God 1765.* Williamsburg: Joseph Royle & Company.

III. OTHER LITERATURE

Adams, Randolph G. *Three Americanists.* Philadelphia: University of Pennsylvania Press, 1939.

Adkins, N. F. *Philip Freneau and the Cosmic Enigma.* New York: New York University Press, 1949.

Baldwin, Alice M. *The New England Clergy and the American Revolution.* Durham: Duke University Press, 1928.

Barr, Mary-Margaret H. *Voltaire in America, 1744–1800.* Baltimore: The Johns Hopkins Press, 1941.

Becker, Carl. *The Declaration of Independence: A Study in the History of Political Ideas.* New York: Harcourt, Brace & Company, 1922.

Benson, Mary S. *Women in Eighteenth-Century America: A Study of Opinion and Social Usage.* New York: Columbia University Press, 1935.

Black, F. G. *The Epistolary Novel in the late Eighteenth Century: A Descriptive and Bibliographical Study.* Eugene: University of Oregon, 1940.

Bowers, Claude G. "Jefferson and the Freedom of the Human Spirit," *Ethics,* LIII (1943).

Bradsher, E. J. *Mathew Carey, Editor, Author and Publisher: A Study in American literary development.* New York: The Columbia University Press, 1912.

——. "A Model American Library of 1793," *The Sewanee Review,* XXIV (1916).

Brigham, Clarence S. *History and Bibliography of American Newspapers, 1690–1820.* 2 vols. Worcester: American Antiquarian Society, 1947.

Brown, Herbert R. *The Sentimental Novel in America, 1789–1860.* Durham: Duke University Press, 1940.

Bruce, W. C. *John Randolph of Roanoke, 1773–1833.* 2 vols. New York: G. P. Putnam's Sons, 1922.

Cabell, N. F., ed. *Early History of the University of Virginia, as contained in the Letters of Thomas Jefferson and Joseph C. Cabell.* Richmond: J. W. Randolph, 1856.

Cambridge History of American Literature. 3 vols. in 1. New York: The Macmillan Company, 1945.

Channing, William Ellery. *Memoir.* 6th ed. 3 vols. Boston: Crosby, Nichols, & Company, 1854.

Chinard, Gilbert. *La Déclaration des Droits de l'Homme et du Citoyen et ses antécédents américains.* Washington: Institut Français de Washington, 1945.

——. *Thomas Jefferson: The Apostle of Americanism,* 2nd ed., revised. Ann Arbor: University of Michigan Press, 1957.

Clark, D. L. *Charles Brockden Brown: A Critical Biography.* New York[?], 1923.

Clark, H. H. "American Literary History and American Literature." In *The Reinterpretation of American Literature,* ed. Norman Foerster. New York: Russell & Russell, 1959.

Clough, Wilson O. *Our long Heritage: Pages from the Books Our Founding Fathers Read.* Minneapolis: University of Minnesota Press, 1955.

Collins, V. L. *President Witherspoon, a biography.* 2 vols. Princeton: Princeton University Press, 1925.

Cometti, Elizabeth. *Jefferson's Ideas on a University Library.* Charlottesville: Tracy W. McGregor Library, University of Virginia, 1950.

Cowie, Alexander. *The Rise of the American Novel.* New York: American Book Co., 1948.

Curti, Merle E. "The Great Mr. Locke: America's Philosopher," *Huntington Library Bulletin,* No. 11, April, 1937.
———. *The Growth of American Thought.* New York: Harper & Brothers, 1943.

Davis, R. B. *Francis Walker Gilmer: Life and Learning in Jefferson's Virginia.* Richmond: The Dietz Press, 1939.

Eiselen, M. R. *Franklin's Political Theories.* Garden City, Doubleday, Doran & Company, Inc., 1928.

Farrand, Max. *The Fathers of the Constitution.* New Haven: Yale University Press, 1921.

Faÿ, Bernard. "La Langue française à Harvard." In *Harvard et la France.* Paris: Edité par les soins de la Revue d'histoire moderne, 1936.
———. *The Revolutionary Spirit in France and America: A Study of the Moral and Intellectual Relations between France and the United States at the End of the Eighteenth Century,* trans. Ramon Guthrie. New York: Harcourt, Brace & Company, 1927.

Fenton, J. F., Jr. *The Theory of the Social Compact and its Influence upon the American Revolution.* N.p., 1891.

Fiedler, Leslie A. *Love and Death in the American Novel.* New York: Criterion Books, 1960.

Fisher, G. P. "Jefferson and the Social Compact Theory," *The Yale Review,* II (1894).

Fiske, John. *The Critical Period of American History, 1783–1789.* Cambridge, Mass.: Riverside Press, 1898.

Ford, Henry Jones. *Alexander Hamilton.* New York: Charles Scribner's Sons, 1925.

Friedenwald, Herbert. *The Declaration of Independence: An*

Interpretation and an Analysis. New York: The Macmillan Company, 1904.

Gallas, K. R. "Un ouvrage faussement attribué à Jean-Jacques Rousseau," *Annales Jean-Jacques Rousseau,* XIII (1920–21).

Ganter, Herbert L. "Jefferson's 'Pursuit of Happiness' and Some Forgotten Men," *The William and Mary Quarterly,* 2nd ser. XVI (1936).

Garland, H. A. *The Life of John Randolph of Roanoke.* 2 vols. New York: D. Appleton & Company, 1851.

Gilman, D. C. *James Monroe.* New York: Houghton, Mifflin & Company, 1898.

Gough, J. W. *The Social Contract: A Critical Study of its Development.* 2nd ed. Oxford: Clarendon Press, 1957.

Guérard, Albert L. *The Life and Death of an Ideal.* London: E. Benn, Ltd., 1929.

Gurn, Joseph. *Charles Carroll of Carrollton, 1737–1832.* New York: P. J. Kenedy & Sons, 1932.

Hansen, A. O. *Liberalism and American Education in the Eighteenth Century.* New York: The Macmillan Company, 1926.

Hart, J. D. *The Popular Book: A History of America's Literary Taste.* New York: Oxford University Press, 1950.

Hastings, Hester. *William Ellery Channing and L'Académie des sciences morales et politiques 1870.* Providence: Brown University Press, 1959.

Havens, George R. "James Madison et la pensée française," *Revue de littérature comparée,* III (1923).

Horton, John T. *James Kent: A Study in Conservatism.* New York: D. Appleton-Century Company, Inc., 1939.

Howard, Leon. *The Connecticut Wits.* Chicago: The University of Chicago Press, 1943.

Hubbell, Jay B. *The South in American Literature, 1607–1900.* Durham: Duke University Press, 1954.

Jaffe, A. H. *Bibliography of French Literature in American Magazines in the Eighteenth Century.* East Lansing: Michigan State College Press, 1951.

Jones, Howard Mumford. *America and French Culture, 1750–1848*. Chapel Hill: The University of North Carolina Press, 1927.

———. "The Importation of French Books in Philadelphia, 1750–1800," *Modern Philology*, XXXII (1934).

———. "The Importation of French Literature in New York City, 1750–1800," *Studies in Philology*, XXVIII (1931).

Joyaux, G. J. "French Thought in American Magazines: 1800–1848." Diss., Michigan State College, 1951.

Kohn, Hans. *The Idea of Nationalism: A Study in its Origins and Background*. New York: The Macmillan Company, 1944.

Lahee, H. C. *Annals of Music in America*. Boston: Marshall Jones Company, 1922.

Leary, Lewis. *That Rascal Freneau: A Study in Literary Failure*. New Brunswick: Rutgers University Press, 1941.

Lichtenberger, André. *Le socialisme au XVIII° siècle*. Paris: F. Alcan, 1895.

Loughrey, Mary E. *France and Rhode Island, 1686–1800*. New York: King's Crown Press, 1944.

Lower Norfolk County Virginia Antiquary, V (1906).

McDermott, John F. *Private Libraries in Creole Saint Louis*. Baltimore: The Johns Hopkins Press, 1938.

McDowell, Tremaine. "Sensibility in the Eighteenth-Century American Novel," *Studies in Philology*, XXIV (1927).

McLaughlin, A. C. "Social Compact and Constitutional Construction," *The American Historical Review*, V (1900).

McMaster, J. B. *The Life and Times of Stephen Girard, Mariner and Merchant*. 2 vols. Philadelphia: J. B. Lippincott Company, 1918.

Martin, Kingsley. *French Liberal Thought in the Eighteenth Century*. Boston: Little, Brown, & Company, 1929.

Miller, Victor C. *Joel Barlow: Revolutionist, London, 1791–92*. Hamburg: Friederichsen, de Gruyter & Company, 1932.

Monthly Criterion, VII (1928).

Morais, Herbert M. *Deism in Eighteenth Century America*. New York: Columbia University Press, 1934.

Mornet, Daniel. "Les Enseignements des bibliothèques privées (1750–1780)," *Revue d'Histoire littéraire de la France,* XVII (1910).

———. *Les Origines intellectuelles de la Révolution française,* 1715–1787. 5th ed. Paris: Librairie Armand Colin, 1954.

Mott, Frank Luther. *Golden Multitudes: The Story of Best Sellers in the United States.* New York: Macmillan Company, 1947.

Mullett, C. F. *Fundamental Law and the American Revolution,* 1760–1776. New York: Columbia University Press, 1933.

Myers, R. M. "The Old Dominion Looks to London," *The Virginia Magazine of History and Biography,* LIV (1946).

Oberholtzer, E. P. *Philadelphia: A History of the City and its People.* 4 vols. Philadelphia: The S. J. Clarke Publishing Company, 1912.

Palmer, R. R. *The Age of the Democratic Revolution: A political History of Europe and America,* 1760–1800. 2 vols. Princeton: Princeton University Press, 1959–64.

Parrington, V. L. *Main Currents in American Thought: an Interpretation of American literature from the beginnings to 1920.* 3 vols. New York: Harcourt, Brace & Company, 1927–30.

Parton, James. *The Life and Times of Aaron Burr . . . ,* enlarged ed. 2 vols. Boston: Ticknor and Fields, 1867.

Paul, Herbert W., ed. *Letters of Lord Acton to Mary, Daughter of the Right Hon. W. E. Gladstone.* London: G. Allen, 1904.

Perry, Ralph Barton. *Puritanism and Democracy.* New York: The Vanguard Press, 1944.

Quincy, Josiah. *The History of Harvard University.* 2 vols. Cambridge, Mass.: J. Owen, 1840.

Raddin, G. G., Jr. *An Early New York Library of Fiction, with a Checklist of the Fiction in H. Caritat's Circulating Library.* New York: The H. W. Wilson Company, 1940.

Ramsay, David. *Memoirs of the Life of Martha Laurens Ramsay . . . .* Philadelphia: James Maxwell, 1811.

Rice, H. C. *Le Cultivateur américain: Etude sur l'Œuvre de*

Saint John de Crèvecœur. In *Bibliothèque de la Revue de littérature comparée*, LXXXVII (1933).

Robinove, Phyllis S. "The Reputation of the Philosophes in France, 1789–1799." Diss., Columbia Univ., 1955.

Roosevelt, Theodore. *Gouverneur Morris*. Boston & New York: Houghton, Mifflin & Company, 1898.

Rossiter, Clinton. *Seedtime of the Republic*. New York: Harcourt, Brace & Company, 1953.

Rovillain, E. E. "Les Bigarures d'un citoyen de Genève (1776–1777)," *Annales Jean-Jacques Rousseau*, XXIII (1934).

Ruplinger, André. *Charles Bordes*. Lyons: A. Rey, 1915.

Schachner, Nathan. *Aaron Burr*. New York: Frederick A. Stokes Company, 1937.

Schinz, Albert. "La Librairie française en Amérique au temps de Washington," *Revue d'histoire littéraire de la France,* XXIV (1917).

———. "Un 'Rousseauiste' en Amérique (*L'Abeille Française,* de Joseph Nancrède)," *Modern Language Notes,* XXXV (1920).

Schlatter, Richard. *Private Property: The History of an Idea.* New Brunswick: Rutgers University Press, 1951.

Scudder, Horace E. *Noah Webster*. New York: Houghton, Mifflin & Company, 1882.

Seeber, Edward D. "The French Theatre in Charleston in the Eighteenth Century," *The South Carolina Historical and Genealogical Magazine*, XLII (1941).

Shearer, J. F. "French and Spanish Works, Printed in Charleston, South Carolina," *The Papers of the Bibliographical Society of America*, XXXIV (1940).

Shera, J. H. *Foundations of the Public Library.* Chicago: University of Chicago Press, 1949.

Shores, Louis. *Origins of the American College Library, 1638–1800.* New York: Barnes & Noble, Inc., 1935.

Skeel, Emily E. F. *Mason Locke Weems: His Works and Ways.* 3 vols. New York, 1929.

Smart, G. K. "Private Libraries in Colonial Virginia," *American Literature,* X (1938).

Sonneck, O. G. *Early Opera in America.* New York: G. Schirmer, 1915.

Steell, W. *Benjamin Franklin of Paris . . . 1776–1785.* New York: Minton, Balch & Company, 1928.

Torrey, Norman L., ed. *Les Philosophes.* New York: Capricorn Books, 1960.

Virginia Magazine of History and Biography, XXIX (1921).

Waldo, Lewis P. *The French Drama in America in the Eighteenth Century.* Baltimore: The Johns Hopkins Press, 1942.

Walsh, C. M. *The Political Science of John Adams: A Study in the Theory of Mixed Government and the Bicameral System.* New York: G. P. Putnam's Sons, 1915.

Warfel, Harry R. *Charles Brockden Brown: American Gothic Novelist.* Gainesville: University of Florida Press, 1949.

Weeks, S. B. *Libraries and Literature in North Carolina in the Eighteenth Century.* In *Annual Report of the American Historical Association for the Year 1895.* Washington: Government Printing Office, 1896.

Wheeler, J. T. "Booksellers and Circulating Libraries in Colonial Maryland," *The Maryland Historical Magazine,* XXXIV (1939).

————. "Reading Interests of Maryland Planters and Merchants 1700–1776," *The Maryland Historical Magazine,* XXXVII (1942).

Whitridge, Arnold. "Brillat-Savarin in America," *The Franco-American Review,* I (1936).

Wiley, Lulu R. *The Sources and Influence of the Novels of Charles Brockden Brown.* New York: Vantage Press, 1950.

William and Mary College Quarterly Historical Magazine, XI (1902–1903).

Wilson, Francis G. *The American Political Mind.* New York: McGraw-Hill Book Company, 1949.

Index